MASTERING the RULES of the GAME

The Merger of Leadership, Perception and Purpose.

Unleash Your Peak C-suite Performance and Win.

DIAN GRIESEL, PH.D.

Copyright © 2025 Dian Griesel.
Headshot Photo Credit: Susan Bowlus
All rights reserved.

No part of this publication may be reproduced, distributed or transmitted in any form or by any means, including photocopying, recording or other electronic or mechanical methods, without the prior written permission of the publisher, except in the case of brief quotations, reviews and other noncommercial uses permitted by copyright law.

ISBN: 9798309586295

Imprint: Independently published

For permissions and any other information, contact:

Perception Dynamics Inc.

212.825.3210

Mastering the Rules of the Game:

The Merger of Leadership, Perception and Purpose.//
Unleash Your Peak C-suite Performance and Win

Disclaimer: A Tale with Fictionalized Names

There are a variety of case studies in this book. Each is an "I was there" window into the real-life, nail-biting, often caffeine-fueled adventures of advising, managing, strategizing and messaging good, bad and downright ugly corporate developments for the best possible outcomes. I've lived through each of these situations and more. Every twist, turn, triumph and "oh no, not that again!" moment shared in these pages happened. The purpose of sharing these abbreviated stories is to provide perspective and insight for your benefit and strategies for your success.

However, to protect the innocent, the guilty, and those who might vehemently deny involvement, all company names, funds, and other parties in these case studies have been *completely fictionalized*. While the lessons, strategies, and outcomes shared on every page are as real as the spreadsheets, results, product failures, corporate CFO accounting missteps, activists and more -- all while I lost many a good night's sleep -- the actual names have been swapped out for pseudonyms, aliases, or just plain fun replacements.

If you think you recognize someone or something, that's purely a coincidence. Or is it? Either way, consider this your friendly reminder: the facts remain true, but the names are where reality takes a creative detour. Enjoy the stories, learn from the strategies, and rest assured -- your secrets (if you were involved) are safe with me. 😉

Contents

Author's Note xi
Introduction xv

Section I: Strategic Vision 1

Chapter 1.   Visionary Leadership: Inspiring Purpose-Driven Growth 3
Chapter 2.   Strategic Thinking: The Bridge Between Vision and Reality 7
Chapter 3.   Maintaining Agility in Dynamic Environments: Leadership in Motion .. 11
Chapter 4.   Aligning with Societal Goals: Building a Brand That Matters 17

Section II: Financial Stewardship 23

Chapter 5.   The Art of Convincing: The Daily Sale & Answering Tough Questions .. 25
Chapter 6.   Capital Allocation and The Leadership Role in Maintaining Financial Health & Sustainable Growth 54
Chapter 7.   Crafting and Sustaining Equity and Debt Strategies for Optimal Financial Health 65
Chapter 8.   Balancing Competing Priorities: Quarterly Earnings vs. Long-Term Goals 72
Chapter 9.   Managing Investor Relations: Building Trust and Navigating Activist Investor Pressure 78
Chapter 10. Ethics in Leadership: Navigating Gray Areas in Corporate Decision-Making 85

Chapter 11. Cultivating Effective Board Relations: Alignment with Independence...93

Chapter 12. Succession Planning: Building a Legacy Through Seamless Leadership Transitions...101

Chapter 13. Transparency is Power: Building Trust and Competitive Advantage...108

Section III: Risk, Resilience and Responsibility...115

Chapter 14. Anticipating Risks and Leading Through Crisis: A Leader's Playbook for Resilience...117

Chapter 15. Cybersecurity in the Boardroom: A Leader's Role in Data Protection and Safeguarding the Future...123

Chapter 16. Leadership in Crisis: Principles for Navigating the Unexpected with Composure and Care...130

Chapter 17. Navigating Climate and Sustainability Risks: Addressing Regulations, Politics, and Activist Shareholders...137

Section IV: Innovation and Adaptation...145

Chapter 18. Leading Digital Transformation: Adapting, Igniting & Driving Technological Innovation for Resilience and Growth...147

Chapter 19. Harnessing AI for Smarter Decisions: A Leader's Guide in the Age of Artificial Intelligence...155

Chapter 20. Balancing Creativity and Execution: Leadership in Structure, Experimentation and Results...163

Section V: People and Culture...169

Chapter 21. Future-Proofing the Workforce: The Leadership Role in HR Strategy and Resilience...171

Chapter 22. Corporate Culture as a Growth Strategy: Igniting Success with Purpose and Passion...176

Chapter 23. Diversity, Equity, and Inclusion: Unlocking the Power of People and Purpose. 182

Chapter 24. Retaining Top Talent: Leadership Strategies to Build Loyalty and Drive Excellence 186

Chapter 25. Leading in a Hybrid Work World: Balancing Flexibility and Accountability for Maximum Impact. 191

Section VI: Communication and Influence 195

Chapter 26. Media Relations in the Digital Age: Mastering the Art of Shaping Public Perception with Visionary Leadership 197

Chapter 27. Becoming an Industry Thought Leader: The Empowering Influence of Authentic Storytelling. 205

Chapter 28. Communicating During a Crisis: How Perceptive Leaders Go Forward with Clarity and Confidence. 215

Chapter 29. Keeping Employees Motivated and Aligned During Times of Change: Perceptive Leadership and Mastering Internal Messaging 223

Section VII: The Private and Personal Side of Leadership 229

Chapter 30. The Loneliness of Leadership: Strategies for Maintaining Perspective and Connection 231

Chapter 31. Maintaining Energy, Building Resilience, and Avoiding Burnout: The Perceptive Leader's Guide to Sustainable Success. 238

Chapter 32. The Power of Continuous Learning: Staying Curious and Adaptive in a Fast-Changing World. 242

Chapter 33. Building Your Legacy: Ensuring Your Impact Endures. 246

Chapter 34. The CEO's Playbook for the Future: Honing Perceptive Talents and Trusting Them 251

About the Author 257

Author's Note

Start Here!

Mastering the leadership game at the highest levels requires a wealth of knowledge and a distinctive blend of focus, resilience, and adaptability. Inspiring others to rally behind your corporate vision is a formidable challenge, and despite being surrounded by people every day, feelings of isolation can creep in. At the Presidential and CEO levels, the weight of decisions that can determine your company's fate rests heavily on your shoulders — often in solitude. You're under the constant glare of your Board of Directors, investor expectations, public scrutiny, and the aspirations of your team. Every yes, no, and maybe hinges on your judgment in one way or another. As you ascend the corporate ladder, the burdens of leadership grow heavier, intensifying feelings of loneliness -- especially if a robust support system is lacking. The demands of leadership extend beyond strategy and financial targets; they delve deep into the personal trials accompanying such immense responsibility.

How do you make decisions when the stakes are seismic? It is not uncommon to wonder how you can maintain clarity and confidence when expected to be unshakable. And who do you turn to when it feels like no one else can truly understand your pressures? Where's the roadmap? Burnout, self-doubt, and the quiet ache of isolation can creep in, undermining even the most capable leaders.

This reality side of leadership often goes unspoken, and if you can relate to this at all, be assured that you are not the only one grappling to find assurance. Many of your peers face similar struggles. I've faced them many times myself and I've spoken with countless leaders who "know the feeling," as well.

When I talk with leaders about mastering the "Rules" of the "Game," I'm not referring to a simple competition or a set of hypothetical business school challenges. "The Game" I am talking about is the high-stakes arena where CEOs and business leaders navigate real-world, complex interplays of perceptions, strategies and outcomes that define success in today's fast-moving, unforgiving markets. It's the intricate chessboard being played by leaders of public and investor-facing companies -- a realm where every move is scrutinized, every decision reverberates, and every misstep can have rippling consequences. 'The Game' is the strategic and emotional battle that leaders face in their quest for success: Mastering it is the key to effective leadership in high-stakes environments.

Excelling in "The Game" requires not just talent but mastery of "The Rules" -- those oft-unwritten principles that dictate the flow of capital, the sway of public opinion, and the behavior of shareholders, stakeholders, and markets. These rules, along with the importance of transparency in communication; the need for adaptability in the face of change; and, the value of ethical decision-making, are anything but static. They shift with market conditions; regulatory landscapes; technological advancements; and, societal expectations. Yet one constant remains: Leaders who learn the rules of the game can anticipate, adapt, and align with these shifting dynamics -- and they are the ones who thrive.

Success in "The Game" hinges on more than operational expertise or financial acumen. It demands a profound perceptiveness -- a sixth sense for understanding how decisions ripple through the network of stakeholders that shape a company's trajectory. When I discuss the dynamics of perception with my clients, I'm referring to the art of learned intuition, including the ability to bring together the power of all of your senses and distinguish between subjective and objective thinking while deeply understanding the impact of conscious and unconscious beliefs. The reason leaders who understand these perception dynamics win more is becausefrom the boardroom to the trading floor, from customers to regulators, every decision is filtered through the lens of human perception. Investors ask, "Can I trust this leadership?" Customers wonder, "Does this brand align with my values?" Employees question, "Is this a company I can believe in?"

Mastering "The Rules" means navigating these myriad layers of perception with strategic clarity and emotional intelligence. CEOs must juggle the relentless demands of securing capital, managing innovation, and maintaining market confidence while anticipating how each action will be interpreted and received. The stakes are amplified in the public eye, where investor relations, media narratives, and marketing strategies converge to create a company's reality – reflecting the cumulative perception held by the masses. Your emotional intelligence is not just a tool, but a powerful weapon in this complex game, empowering you to control the narrative and build confidence.

The Human Side of Leadership

"The 'Game' also tends to be both intensely personal and often very public. And, this is where much of my insight comes into play. For over 30 years, I've advised almost 400 C-suite leaders of publicly traded companies, venture capital firms, and select individuals, helping them navigate the visible and invisible challenges of "The Game." Through my dual expertise as a Perception Analyst and Hypnotherapist, with extensive knowledge and experience with corporate governance and regulations, I've been able to address both the professional and personal aspects of leadership. I understand the personal sacrifices and public scrutiny, and I'm here to add more knowledge that may help while acknowledging and validating your experience.

About Me...

I've successfully played "The Game" and invested decades in mastering its "Rules." My life's work, leading my investor and public relations company where I was responsible for generating multi-millions in revenues to being able to pay out over $40 million in employee salaries over 18 years before selling to a publicly traded company, has taught me a lot. This journey was not without its compromises: I worked far beyond a 40-hour week including plenty of weekends and holidays with my CEO clients who needed a thought partner, sounding board, and strategist during negotiations, decision-making, and subsequent messaging of disclosure announcements -- all that while staying married and raising our two children. Cumulatively this has given me a deep personal understanding of the unique complexities leaders must balance, and I am here to share these insights with you.

Within these pages you will find a range of practical considerations and strategies that apply to every leader who aspires to grow their company within the financial markets. I've curated them from my many years of advising CEOs and boards on not only their day-to-day challenges but, particularly, from strategizing after uncovering perceptions that held the potential to significantly impact the outcomes of things like crises (good or bad), performance issues, product updates (and failures), fundraises, transactions, acquisitions, divestitures, leadership transitions (voluntary and not so), board conflicts, plus all kinds of Securities and Exchange Commission (SEC), Federal Trade Commission (FTC) and Food and Drug Administration (FDA) and Department of Defense (DoD) disclosure issues – to name a few of the acronym departments I've interacted with, shoulder-to-shoulder with my clients.

I trust that you'll find these pages empowering. I hope that each section will equip you to better play 'The Game' as you further master its Rules. By doing so, you can leave a remarkable legacy of lasting impact, inspiring others to follow in your footsteps. And, if along the way you decide you need a good confidant to bounce your ideas and strategize with – give me a call.

Introduction

Leadership is a calling. A responsibility is as profound as it is transformational. When you step into the role of CEO of a public company -- or prepare to take that leap -- you enter a realm where the stakes are high, the challenges are immense, and the opportunities are boundless. You'll be responsible for shaping a vision that cuts through the noise, galvanizes teams, and builds trust with people you may never meet. While inevitable storms rage, you'll still be expected to be the calm, guiding voice that instills confidence in shareholders, stakeholders, employees, the media, and communities alike.

In the high-stakes arena of public companies, one element reigns supreme: Perception. It's the multi-faceted lens through which every decision, action and word will be scrutinized by your "publics" as they analyze and process your narratives. Perception, formed at the intersection of thoughts and emotions, is the key to shaping the beliefs that define how your leadership is assessed. Inhabiting the C-suite, the perceptions held by others are amplified and magnified -- reflecting how you're shaping your reputation; defining your credibility; adding value; and bringing purpose and potential to your entire organization.

Perception is the currency of leadership. It determines whether the world buys into your vision, worthiness, and trustworthiness.

Balancing the Unbalanceable

For a CEO, leadership often means balancing what feels unbalanceable: Delivering results while staying true to purpose; protecting competitive advantage while embracing transparency; inspiring a diverse array of stakeholders -- including investors, analysts, employees, partners and communities -- while making tough decisions that won't always win applause or initially create favorable perceptions. Leadership in the public arena is rarely black and white. It's a kaleidoscope of nuance, resilience, perspectives, and perceptions where words and actions are carefully analyzed.

Among the most powerful words you'll wield are "Yes," "No," and "Maybe. Let me think about it." When used as deliberate and complete sentences, these phrases can potentially shape businesses as well as lives, relationships, and futures. Perceptive leaders understand the profound power inherent in these words, using them as tools of empowerment, boundaries, and contemplation. Mastering their use is a hallmark of intentional leadership -- guiding teams, shaping strategies, and influencing outcomes precisely and purposefully.

To say "Yes" as a leader is to embrace opportunity, foster growth, and cultivate connection. It signifies readiness to commit and act, not just individually but collectively. Exceptional leaders understand the gravity of "Yes" and wield it with clarity and alignment with their vision and values. Their "Yes" is not impulsive but an intentional declaration grounded in preparation, resourcefulness, and foresight. A purposeful "Yes" ignites collaboration, inspires trust, and paves the way for transformation -- both for their teams and the organizations they lead.

"No" is the cornerstone of boundary-setting in leadership. It protects time, energy, and focus, ensuring that priorities and values remain uncompromised. Leaders who confidently say "No" do so with an awareness that it is not a rejection of others but an affirmation of what truly matters. A well-placed "No" safeguards against distractions and overcommitment, allowing leaders to channel their efforts toward meaningful goals and sustainable growth. Delivered with respect and conviction, "no" becomes an act of mutual respect, fostering trust by demonstrating clear priorities and integrity, providing a sense of security and focus.

The often-overlooked power of "Maybe. Let me think about it." is a profound tool of reflective leadership. In a fast-paced world that demands immediate decisions, perceptive leaders recognize the strength of pausing. This thoughtful approach allows space for emotions to settle, facts to be gathered, and intuition to surface. "Maybe. Let me think about it." embodies patience, mindfulness, and strategic discernment, ensuring decisions are made with both rational analysis and emotional intelligence. By embracing the pause, leaders demonstrate humility and wisdom, empowering themselves to make balanced, well-informed choices, and fostering a sense of wisdom and thoughtfulness.

The mastery of these three phrases -- "Yes," "No," and "Maybe. Let me think about it." – helps to define perceptive leadership in all aspects of both your professional and also personal life. Together, they form a language of empowerment that enables leaders to navigate complexity with grace, intentionality, and clarity.

Saying "Yes" to aligned opportunities, "No" to distractions, and "Maybe" when deeper consideration is required creates a framework for authentic, purposeful leadership.

Ultimately, the power of these words lies not only in their utterance but in the wisdom of their application.

The Balancing Act of Public Leadership

As you can see, being the leader of a company isn't just about what's on the balance sheet. It's about thoughtfully processing countless decisions while managing an assortment of factors that will define your success. In no small way, this includes finding ways to better connect with:

- **Shareholders** who want to trust you with their investments while expecting full transparency as you navigate risks and growth.
- **Employees** who look to you for stability, clarity and hope -- even in uncertain times.
- **Partners and customers** who may bring demands that seem unreasonable or unimaginable but expect you to fulfill them -- or find someone else who will.

- **Communities and customers** who are increasingly demanding to see the "heart" of your company -- not just its financial performance.
- **Regulators** who will scrutinize, inspect and audit every move your company makes.
- **The Media**, which will report -- accurately, inaccurately, or incite-fully (though not necessarily insight-fully) -- on every detail of your leadership, from decisions and financial reports to community actions and employee dynamics. Expect headlines of any missteps to scream in bold font, while corrections or clarifications rarely reach even the back pages.

Throughout this book, I'll collectively call them your **"Publics"** – namely, a composite of all of the above. It will be your "publics" that will amplify every success or stumble in ways you can't predict. Today's triumph will be celebrated for a fleeting moment before the inevitable "What's next?" arrives.

While headlines focus on quarterly results or high-profile deals, the real work of leadership is often accomplished in the quieter moments -- when decisions are made with intention and a long-term perspective.

Why Perception Is Your Secret Asset

In the realm of leadership, as we'll explore throughout these pages, perception is everything. It's not just a public relations tool -- it's a powerful energy force. Perception can be managed and doing so (or not) shapes how people feel about you, your company, products, services, and your mission. It becomes the force of "The Market:" a complex public merger of thoughts, emotions, and beliefs -- which ultimately reflect corporate valuations.

How you manage perceptions -- both your own and those of others -- doesn't just influence your company's reputation; it shapes its trajectory. Perceptive leadership inspires customer loyalty, builds investor confidence, and creates a ripple effect that impacts markets, communities and beyond. Understanding and leveraging this power transforms good leaders into extraordinary ones.

Because here's the truth: perceptive leadership isn't for the faint of heart. It demands the intention to stay attuned and ask the questions even when you might not like the answers; the resilience to withstand pressure; the courage to stand firm in uncertainty; and the wisdom to pivot when necessary because you have more information than before.

Your Blueprint for Inspired Leadership

This book isn't about telling you what you already know -- it's about helping you elevate, refine, and apply what you know and more. It's also about introducing and reminding you of the many ways you can use your influence to build bridges, break barriers, and leave a legacy of clarity, confidence and purpose. Because at the end of the day, perceptive leadership isn't just about what you do -- it's about who you become along the way.

This book is also here to remind you that you're not alone. No matter how heavy the burden of leadership may feel, you have what it takes to carry it. You are resilient, you are capable, and you are more than equipped to handle the challenges that come your way.

If you've ever prepared for a tough call -- balancing the demands of shareholders, employees and boards while staying true to your vision -- this book is for you. It's not a lecture. It's not a checklist. It's a guide you can turn to when the stakes are high, the pressure is unrelenting, and the answers aren't clear.

8 Ways This Book Will Help You

1. Expect Practical Advice You Can Use Right Away

Leadership isn't theoretical -- it's real, gritty, and fast-paced. Each chapter in this book is short and bulleted for a reason: So, you can dive in, jiggle your memory, grab a bit of insight you may need and get back to leading. It's written with your packed calendar in mind.

2. It Acknowledges the Challenges Only You Know

Seriously, few outside of the C-suite truly understand the unique pressure of being a public company CEO unless they've lived it. The constant scrutiny. The impossible expectations. This book doesn't gloss over those realities. Instead, it meets you right where you are, with tools to navigate the noise and focus on what matters.

3. A Roadmap for Every Side of Leadership

Leadership isn't just about numbers or strategy. It's about people. It's about purpose. It's about making decisions that align with who you are and the impact you want to leave behind. From governance to innovation, risk management to personal resilience, this book covers it all -- because you're leading on every front, whether you realize it or not.

4. Space to Pause and Reflect

You move fast, but sometimes, the quiet moments of reflection hold the greatest power. This book gives you those moments -- and encourages you to find more of them. Real-world examples and reflection questions are here to nudge you toward growth, deeper self-awareness, and a clearer sense of your impact -- not just on the company but the world around you.

5. Balancing the Short-Term Grind with Long-Term Vision

You know the drill: quarterly earnings dominate the conversation, but you're also the keeper of the long-term vision. This book helps you hold both realities in balance so you can lead with integrity today while building something that will last for decades.

6. Preparing for the Curveballs
The business world doesn't stand still, and neither can you. Technology, regulations, and societal expectations -- are all shifting fast. This book doesn't just address what's happening now; it anticipates what's coming and helps you stay ahead of the game.

7. Encouraging You to Think About Your Legacy
You'll be reminded to step back momentarily: Why did you want to be a CEO? What drives you? This book invites you to reconnect with those deeper questions. Yes, you're managing a business -- but you're also building a legacy. One that's defined by more than profits. A legacy that speaks to your purpose, values, and the mark you want to leave on the world.

8. A CEO's Companion, Whenever You Need It
You're busy. That's why each chapter is designed to stand alone. Pick it up quietly in your office or while waiting for your next meeting. It's there for you when you need it, no matter what's on your plate.

This book isn't about telling you how to do your job -- you've got the expertise and that's why YOU are the Boss. It's here to remind you of your capabilities, to guide you through the pressures with wisdom, and to show you what it means to lead with smarts and heart. Because here's the truth: being a CEO isn't just about steering the ship. It's about inspiring the people on board, weathering the storms, and remembering that the journey is about more than just the destination.

You've got this. And this book has your back.

Section I

Strategic Vision

Chapter 1

Visionary Leadership: Inspiring Purpose-Driven Growth

Becoming a perceptive leader starts with understanding how your ideas and beliefs merge to form your leadership operating system. So, let's start by contemplating (maybe even reconsidering) your vision. Not the kind of vision written on a piece of paper and forgotten in some corner of a strategic plan, but the kind that lights a fire of inspiration. The vision you share makes people want to roll up their sleeves and give their best because they see themselves as an important player in the story that you are telling. The kind of vision that inspires others to help you achieve your goals – whether through investments, connections, time, sharing or any other way they can assist and elevate your ultimate success.

As a CEO, your role in shaping a purpose-driven vision is more than just a roadmap -- it's the heartbeat of your organization. It's your energy that connects today's actions with tomorrow's possibilities, inspiring teams and stakeholders to move forward purposefully. A strong vision doesn't just guide -- it galvanizes loyalty.

The Art of Crafting Vision

Great leaders don't just set goals. They paint a picture of what's possible. They see gaps and find ways to fill them. They imagine the kind of world their organization could help create and invite others to join them in making it happen. This kind of leadership, this kind of vision, isn't only about spreadsheets or pie charts but rather the story of having heart and imagination.

A few things make a corporate vision truly impactful:

- **It is Purpose-Driven:** Why does your company exist? What's the greater good you're striving for beyond profit? Whether championing sustainability, revolutionizing an industry, or enriching your customers' lives, a purpose-driven vision gives people a reason to care.
- **It is a Stretch – Not a Fantasy:** A vision should feel like a stretch, not a fantasy. The best visions make people say, "That's bold, but I can see how we'll get there."
- **It is Collaborative:** A vision created in isolation falls flat. You gain depth, richness, and buy-in when you gather a collective of perspectives and invite others to contribute their ideas. Yes, you make the ultimate decisions. But you may be losing much that you don't even realize if you're not one to consider ideas and suggestions from others.

Living the Vision

Here's the truth: A vision isn't worth much if it's merely stuck in a slide deck. It has to be lived, breathed, and woven into every part of your company, from team meetings to casual conversations, quarterly updates and email signatures. Here's how the best leaders make that happen:

- **Keep It Front and Center:** Your vision should be everywhere -- in team meetings, casual conversations, quarterly updates, and email signatures. Repetition isn't just helpful; it's essential.

- **Walk the Talk:** Your actions are your loudest communication tool. Let your vision shine through when you make decisions, prioritize initiatives, or interact with your team. People will believe in your words when they see you living them.
- **Turn Vision Into Action:** A vision without actionable goals is a dream. Break it down into milestones your team can rally around. Every small win reinforces the belief that the vision is within reach.
- **Empower Your People:** You're not the sole keeper of the vision. Your role is to inspire and empower others to make it their own as well. When your team sees how each individual's work contributes to the bigger picture, magic happens.

Inspiring Connection and Commitment

The beauty of a purpose-driven vision, designed with the power of perception in mind, is its magnetism. It not only pulls in talented, passionate people who want to be part of something bigger but also builds loyalty among stakeholders who see the impact of your work beyond financial returns.

When you articulate and embody a clear, powerful vision, you're not just setting direction for your Company's growth and success, but creating momentum to get there faster. You're building an organization that moves as one, fueled by shared purpose and belief.

A Legacy That Lasts

At its core, visionary leadership isn't just about guiding your company toward success. It's about your significant role in inspiring belief in a future that matters. It's about creating a legacy -- not just of profits, but of purpose. A strong vision endures. It grows with the company, shapes its culture, and sustains it through challenges and change. We'll be exploring this later, in detail.

But for now, step into your role as a visionary leader. Dream big. Speak boldly. And never underestimate the transformative power of a purpose-driven vision to not only revolutionize your organization but also potentially change the world.

Chaper 2

Strategic Thinking: The Bridge Between Vision and Reality

Let's face it -- dreaming big is the fun part of being the CEO of any company. But turning those dreams into reality? That's where the magic happens. Strategic thinking is the engine that takes a CEO's grand vision and turns it into something tangible, achievable and extraordinary. It's not just about thinking ahead; it's about thinking smart -- balancing innovation with practicality and ambition with execution. For instance, consider a CEO who strategically aligns their vision with market realities, turning big goals into bite-sized steps, adapting on the fly, making every resource count, balancing boldness with caution, building bridges with stakeholders, keeping an eye on the long game, and staying curious and open to change.

This may be you already. And, it can be you starting now. Here's how strategic thinking empowers you to lead with clarity and confidence.

Aligning Vision with Market Realities

A bold vision is exciting, but it only works if it's grounded in reality. Perceptive, strategic thinking is your lens for assessing the competitive landscape, spotting industry trends and identifying those golden opportunities hiding in plain sight. It's the discipline that ensures your vision isn't just a wish list but a roadmap rooted in your company's strengths and the realities of the marketplace.

▮ Turning Big Goals into Bite-Sized Steps

Vision can feel overwhelming if you don't break it down. Perceptive, strategic thinkers know how to translate lofty ambitions into manageable milestones, that give you a sense of control and accomplishment – while also serving as a "milestone checklist" for your various stakeholders and shareholders. Defining a bite-size visionary leadership plan is about creating a clear path forward so your team and others involved aren't just inspired -- they're empowered to act and engage step-by-step, toward the bigger picture.

▮ Adapting on the Fly

The world doesn't sit still, and neither should your strategy. Strategic thinking is your compass when the winds shift -- whether a competitor's entry into your industry sector, a new technology disrupting your industry, a sudden regulatory change, or evolving customer needs. Strategic thinking (like these pages will introduce and review) gives you the agility to pivot without losing sight of where you're headed, and it's crucial in managing change effectively.

▮ Making Every Resource Count

Time, money, talent and technology are all precious, and strategic thinking is how you use them wisely. It's about making choices that align with your long-term vision, avoiding distractions, and staying laser-focused on what truly matters. When every resource is tied to the bigger goal, you create momentum that's impossible to stop.

▮ Balancing Boldness with Caution

Leadership requires courage, but it also requires calculated risk. Strategic thinking lets you evaluate opportunities clearly, weighing potential rewards against the risks. It's the art of taking bold steps while planning for contingencies -- because real growth happens when you're willing to stretch, but not snap.

Building Bridges with Stakeholders

No vision succeeds in isolation. Strategic thinkers know the importance of collaboration -- engaging your board, employees, investors, and even customers. Involving others creates a collective energy and shared purpose that propels your vision forward.

Keeping an Eye on the Long Game

Quarterly results matter, sure. But the accurate measure of success lies in your ability to consider the long term. Quarters and related stock charts rarely go straight up. Strategic thinking gives you the patience and perspective to prioritize sustainable growth over quick wins, ensuring your leadership legacy stands the test of time.

Staying Curious and Open to Change

The best leaders are lifelong learners, as we'll explore further in this book. Strategic thinking means staying curious, staying informed and staying ahead -- all of which help to ensure you're always one step ahead of the competition. It's about embracing new ideas, exploring what's next, and using innovation as your edge. When you're constantly growing, so is your company.

Strategic thinking is where the rubber meets the road. It's the force that turns vision into action, inspiration into impact. It's not just about anticipating challenges: It's about embracing them, adapting to them and thriving because of them – even those challenges you would have preferred to have skipped!

You're unstoppable when you combine the clarity of a strong vision with the discipline of strategic thinking. You are equipped to create an organization that's not just prepared for the future -- but shaping it.

So, lead boldly, think strategically and remember: Every day you are at the helm of a company, you're not just managing a company but crafting a legacy by your vision, choices and example.

Chapter 3

Maintaining Agility in Dynamic Environments: Leadership in Motion.

Let's talk about agility. Not the kind that's about flashy, quick moves, but the deep, steady, intentional kind that helps you stay grounded while everything around you is shifting. In today's fast-paced business world, agility isn't optional. It's what separates the leaders who thrive from the ones who simply survive.

The reality is this: Markets change. Customers change. Technology changes. And as a CEO, you're tasked with navigating all of it -- balancing the need to move fast with the discipline to stay strategic. Agility isn't just about reacting; it's about perceptively responding with wisdom, resilience and focus.

So, how do you lead with that kind of adaptability? It starts with a mindset, and it's supported by the right tools and frameworks.

Embracing Agile Thinking

Agility isn't just a buzzword -- it's a way of leading with flexibility and intention. Choosing to work on being more agile works because it is foundationally built on empowering yourself and those you lead to break down big challenges into smaller, manageable steps. Here's why it works:

- Agility allows for quick decisions that can be tested and refined in real-time.
- Agility brings diverse minds together, as it encourages collaboration across teams and departments.
- It keeps your focus on the people who matter most -- your customers -- ensuring that every move you make aligns with their needs.

Agility isn't about rushing; it's about moving with purpose and precision.

Think Ahead with Scenario Planning

"What if?" Is a question commonly asked by every great leader. Scenario planning is your chance to look around the corner, anticipate what might come next and prepare your team. When you imagine different possibilities -- good, bad, or somewhere in between -- you give yourself the power to respond and not just react. Reactions are very often nothing more than "re-actions," which are the result of pulling out old files and re-acting past situations vs. accurately assessing the current issue at hand. Learning to ask, "What if?" helps everyone feel more prepared for the future.

With scenario planning, you:

- Stay proactive in uncertain times, becoming more ready for disruptions before they happen.
- Balance risks and opportunities with a clear-eyed view of what's possible.

- Equip your team with confidence, knowing they've already contributed to mapping out strategies for the future. So you have both "buy-in" and a plan, if necessary.

Innovate Like a Startup

Big organizations often feel like they're moving through molasses -- but there are ways to manage this sensation. By reintroducing and adopting applicable aspects of a lean start-up approach, even the largest companies can act with the creativity and speed of a small, scrappy team. This approach focuses on your "minimum viable product," testing it quickly, learning from it, and refining it as you go. The beauty of this approach is that it encourages you to not be afraid to fail small and fast. Knowing that every stumble leads to smarter solutions helps you conserve resources by investing only in what truly adds value, and it keeps the spark of innovation alive, no matter how large your organization becomes.

Here's the beauty of maintaining a lean start-up approach:

- You're not afraid to fail small and fast; knowing every stumble leads to smarter solutions.
- You conserve resources by investing only in what truly adds value.
- You keep the spark of innovation alive, no matter how large your organization becomes.

Solve Big Problems, Fast

Whether launching a product, testing a new idea, or solving a complex issue, you might like to try the SPRINT framework as it brings the right people together, forces quick decisions, and gets results, giving you a sense of control and efficiency.

Basically, it emphasizes rapid iteration, collaboration and user feedback, making it particularly useful in fast-paced environments with limited time and resources. It encourages teams to move quickly from problem identification to solution testing, fostering innovation and effective problem-solving.

Here's how it breaks down.

> **S: Specify the Goal:** Clearly define the objective or problem to be solved.
>
> **P: Plan the Approach:** Develop a step-by-step plan, outline key actions, assign roles and allocate resources.
>
> **R: Research and Resources:** Gather necessary information, analyze data, and identify tools or resources required for success.
>
> **I: Implement the Plan:** Execute the plan with focus and commitment, following the agreed steps.
>
> **N: Navigate Challenges:** Monitor progress, address obstacles and adapt the approach as needed to stay on track.
>
> **T: Test and Iterate:** Evaluate results, refine processes and make improvements to achieve the best possible outcome.

While this is a 6-Step approach to problem-solving, remember the acronym is SPRINT! It's not designed to be a 26-mile marathon – but a quick way to coordinate, collaborate, test and innovate. It works because it pushes teams to act decisively, avoiding analysis paralysis. It values cross-functional collaboration, drawing on the wisdom of diverse perspectives. And, lastly, it turns ideas into reality -- *fast* ... or not!

Set Goals That Move You Forward

Agility isn't about winging it. It's about staying aligned on your objectives while being flexible about how you achieve them. That's where stating Objectives and Key Results (OKRs) come in. These help you focus on what matters most, track progress, and pivot when needed.

Defining objectives and key results in greater clarity and alignment across your organization is paramount so everyone keeps rowing in the same direction. It also establishes a rhythm for regular reflection. This can further help you as a leader to adjust as the world changes around you. Whether you recognize it or not, every part of your world -- employees, clients, partners, regulators, end users, investors and everyone else somehow connected or interacting with your company is changing. THAT is a forever guarantee!

Fostering an Agile Culture

Here's the secret: Agility isn't just about processes -- it's about people. The best frameworks in the world won't work without a culture that embraces adaptability, innovation and open communication.

As a CEO, you set the tone. So how do you build agility into your organization? Here's where it starts:

- Empowering your team to think creatively and take ownership.
- Creating a space where ideas flow freely, and feedback is valued.
- By celebrating flexibility, recognizing those who adapt and thrive in the face of change.

The Agility Mindset

At its core, agility is about leading with openness, curiosity and courage. It's about committing to learning -- not just from success but from failure, too. It's about staying calm in the face of chaos, knowing you have the tools and mindset to guide your organization through whatever comes next.

Because here's a big truth: Agility isn't just a strategy. It's a survival skill. And for the leaders who embrace it, it's the foundation of lasting success.

So, stay open. Stay adaptable. And lead with the confidence that, no matter how dynamic the environment, you're ready for it.

Chapter 4

Aligning with Societal Goals: Building a Brand That Matters

Let's pause momentarily and reflect: Why do people choose certain brands? Sure, price and quality matter, but in today's world, the heart of the decision often lies more profoundly in values, purpose and trust. Consumers, employees, and investors aren't just looking for products or services anymore; they're seeking alignment with companies that stand for something bigger. It's a whole new complicated reality of running a public company that you'll have to acknowledge for ongoing viability.

The upside is this: As a CEO, you have a powerful opportunity to build a brand that succeeds financially and resonates emotionally. By aligning with societal goals -- in whatever way they're being packaged by politicians, on college campuses or by the media -- whether it's sustainability, social justice, ethical leadership or the next buzz word that you'll be held accountable to uphold -- you're not just strengthening your brand; you're creating a legacy that inspires loyalty, trust, and respect.

The New Landscape of Brand Equity

The concept of brand equity has evolved. It's no longer just about being reliable or delivering great customer service. Today, brand equity has morphed into something that is quite possibly undefinable and, often, an altogether seemingly impossible, illogical standard. Yet, as CEO, you have to deal with it. And, your scorecard will be determined by how well your company aligns with the values and priorities of the people who engage with it. (Note: I never said being a CEO would be easy!)

Consumers are paying attention to how you treat the planet, your people, and what you stand for. Employees want to work for companies that make them proud. Some investors are looking for organizations that balance profit with purpose. Regulators sometimes even demand this while creating all kinds of hoops you will be required to jump through and prove that you did so in your annual reports. Politicians complicate the landscape further by scapegoating companies and their leaders – often only as an attempt to win headlines, that will not necessarily win votes, but will nonetheless deliver plenty of aggravation for targeted CEOs or industries. These shifts in what defines your brand equity cannot be ignored (even though it is very tempting!) Consider all of this to be a call to action for leaders: An invitation to rethink not just what your company(ies) do but why they do it.

Why Aligning with Societal Goals Matters

Let me just say, because I'm pretty candid – sometimes the only reason some of what seems to be non-sensical "matters" is purely this: Because it does and you don't have a choice. And, because it is-what-it-is and you don't hold the power to set ALL "the Rules." However -- you do hold the power to define many of the Rules. So, let's look at why aligning with the B I G picture is ultimately the way to go.

Aligning your Company, with whatever the societal goal of the year is, matters because…

You might gain more loyal customers, who feel connected to you in trust. When your brand aligns with societal goals, it forges an emotional bond with consumers. They see you as more than a company: Now you're viewed as a partner in building a better world. And this loyalty? It's not just a passing phase. It endures, even when competitors try to lure them away.

Engaged Employees Who Believe in the Mission. People want to do meaningful work. When employees see their efforts contributing to something bigger -- something that aligns with their values -- they appear to be more likely to show up with passion, creativity and commitment. And guess what? They stick around longer, too.

Investor Confidence in Your Vision. Some investors aren't just chasing quick returns anymore. They want quick returns and more! Their charters specifically focus on investing in companies that balance financial success with responsibility. Companies that embrace environmental, social and governance (ESG) principles are in vogue and may attract capital from those who care about a particular long-term impact.

A Unique Identity in a Crowded Market. Let's face it -- competition is fierce. Aligning with societal goals may add to your arsenal for setting your brand apart. It creates aspects of a story that consumers want to be part of, a narrative that inspires trust and preference. Purpose can become your unique identifier in a sea of sameness.

Resilience in Times of Crisis. When you've built a reputation for doing good, people may be more likely to stand by you during tough times. That goodwill -- earned through consistent, authentic alignment with societal goals could become your safety net when the unexpected happens.

How to Lead with a Policy of Purpose

Aligning with societal goals isn't just about putting out a press release or updating your website. It's about weaving the purpose you have defined into your company's fabric. Shareholders and Stakeholders are not stupid. If you think you can fool them – you are on a dangerous route, proceeding at your own peril. This is a bad idea. Instead, follow the steps below.

Start with Authentic Goals: Look inward. What values define your company? What societal issues align with your mission? Make a list. Ask your team. The answers will guide you toward goals that feel real and resonate in a deep, genuine way.

Integrate Purpose into Strategy: Purpose shouldn't be an afterthought. Rather, if you don't want to be unfavorably called out in the "Court of Public Opinion" (Think of this as any form of commentary in traditional or social media!) be realistic and very clear as to how you can realistically incorporate and integrate your newly defined purpose as a guiding force behind your decisions; the shaper of your priorities; and, the reflection in every aspect of your strategy.

Collaborate for Greater Impact: You don't have to go it alone. If you're struggling with this "purpose" concept, consider partnering with nonprofits, communities and even other companies. Such alliances can set a social tone and also offer the added benefit of amplifying your reach as you show your commitment by acting collectively. There's nothing wrong with this strategy: Done right, it's a form of investing in your Company image and future. Every sponsorship you've ever seen – from F1 race cars to sports arenas to events and more -- is built on this premise.

Communicate with Honesty: People can spot "greenwashing" a mile away. Greenwashing is a marketing tactic certain companies mistakenly use in an attempt to mislead consumers into thinking their products, goals or policies are environmentally friendly. Modern consumers and investors proudly think of themselves as detectives. They'll forever be looking for misleading claims, lack of evidence, selective disclosures, overused buzzwords, ambiguous labeling, false certifications and outright lies. Wise CEOs are transparent about their efforts, successes, challenges, and plans for growth. Honesty builds trust. "Actions speak louder than words," said somebody.

Inspire Your Team: Purpose starts with people. Engage your employees, invite their ideas, and recognize their contributions to the company's mission. When they believe in the "why," they'll move mountains for the "how." Share responsibility. If your employees say they want to work at a "greener" company – remember, you can always propose community-building projects that clean up neighborhoods, parks or beaches.

▮ *A Legacy of Impact*

Here's the thing we'll wrap this up with: Aligning with societal goals isn't just good for business. It's good for the soul of your company. It's about creating something bigger than yourself -- contributing to a better world and inspiring those who walk through your doors.

As a CEO, you have the power to lead with purpose, to build a brand that people believe in, and to create a legacy that lasts. Because in the end, the most successful companies aren't just the ones that make money. They're the ones that also figure out big and small ways to make a difference.

Section II
Financial Stewardship

Chapter 5

The Art of Convincing: The Daily Sale & Answering Tough Questions

When an investment banker or fund manager steps into the due diligence process, the room transforms into a stage for probing questions, meticulous scrutiny, and the relentless pursuit of clarity. Every presentation, every line in the financial statements, every forecast in the business plan, and every syllable in the executive pitch becomes subject to analysis. Their goal isn't just to uncover who you are and the story your company is telling -- but to validate credibility and potential for exciting value creation.

What makes your company worth representing? Why should a financial professional risk their reputation or capital for your vision? These are the implicit questions behind every inquiry, and answering them requires meticulous preparation, unwavering transparency, and a profound understanding of your business from every angle. From the granular details of your financial health to the broader strokes of your market strategy, fund managers and investment bankers will always be seeking assurances that your vision and business plans align with their standards for risk and return.

This chapter is designed with a three-fold purpose.

1st: Because perceptive leadership starts with asking the tough questions – you find an internal due diligence questionnaire for yourself and your board members to answer.

2nd: We'll look at improving your pitch and the ways you can grab interest (and money!) from any investor or partner, and then…

3rd: So you can manage the external due diligence process with greater confidence, we will address key "must haves" in your corporate presentation, while I'll also provide a comprehensive list of the critical questions and concerns you should expect as they can shape the outcome of your engagement and/or relationships with potential investors or representatives.

Whether it's about your management cohesive nature, your company's growth trajectory, it's operational resilience, or competitive differentiation, we'll explore a variety of key focus areas and provide actionable insights to help you assess and then articulate your value proposition convincingly.

The Internal Management & Board Due Diligence Exercise

This is an optional but worthy exercise. It will absolutely elevate your perception as it relates to how you, your key leadership and your board members are aligned with thoughts and feelings about your Company -- or not.

To proceed, copy these pages (Yes, you have my permission to copy this section for your internal use only.) Ask each member of your management team and board to complete the questions. The ultimate answers will help you determine how in line the perspectives of the various management members are, and how cohesive you are as a group. This exercise comes with two predictions:

1. It is highly unlikely that all management participants will record equal test scores.
2. The disparity of answers will create some lively internal discussions.

Feeling brave? Give it a try and have your officers, team leaders and board members do likewise.

STRATEGY MODEL

**Does the company have a compelling strategy based
on the current state of its business?**

Vision (Circle the number that applies for each.)

• The Company has a clear, breakthrough vision that can create distinctive advantage

    0 = Can't define it
    1 = Management team can define it but can't agree on it
    3 = Management can articulate and agree on a common vision
    5 = Customers/Competitors/Investors have a clear perception

• The Company can define its market segments clearly

    0 = can't define it
    1 = partially defined
    2 = has defined several viable markets but can't decide on one
    5 = specific markets are defined, are viable, company has specific market knowledge

• The market segments are growing? How fast is the demand for the Company's product(s) within the market segments growing?

    0 = no growth
    1 = don't know
    3 = 10% growth
    5 = >20% growth

- The Company can achieve annual revenues > $200 million by capturing 10% of the market

    0 = 75% market share needed
    1 = 50% market share needed
    3 = 25% market share needed
    5 = 10% market share needed

- The Company has a plan, being executed, to capture 10% of its target market in three years

    0 = no plan
    1 = plan concept
    3 = plan defined, documented being validated that it will meet the timeframe
    5 = plan being executed and the company is confident the plan will meet the 3 year timeframe

- The Company knows what the primary alternatives re to its product(s) and why prospects will choose their product over those alternatives.

    0 = we have no competitors/alternatives
    1 = we can list most common industry competitors
    3 = can list specific competitors/alternatives and know a little about how to compete against them.
    5 = we can describe both competitors/alternatives and common substitutes in detail and clearly understand win/loss situations. We understand which three competitors we must focus on beating.

- The primary differentiator of the company (brand or products) is clear and compelling

    0 = no consistent internal view
    1 = 1 or 2 employees can articulate it
    3 = management and employees can articulate it
    5 = management, the board and customers can articulate it

Business Model or Tipping Point: Does Company have a core proven business model?

- The company can clearly define its primary larger customers / key needs, secondary customers, and customers it will not serve

    0 = no target customer definition
    1 = we can describe the target
    3 = we can describe the target, secondary customers and non customers
    5 = we can define all primary customers in detail specifically, or with demographics/behaviors

- Customer benefits from the products are clear and compelling

    0 = no benefits
    1 = benefits are not unique
    3 = the company can articulate unique benefits
    5 = the company and its customers can articulate the unique benefits

- Can the company show proof of customer acceptance through a sustainable and growing customer/revenue base?

    0 = net decline in customers
    1 = 10% net new customers in last year
    3 = 10% net new customers in last 6 months
    5 = 10% net new customers in last month

- Does the company have a repeatable, profitable customer acquisition strategy that exponentially grows its customer base?

    0 = not demonstrated ability to acquire new customers
    1 = makes sales, but not predictable, cannot define sales model
    3 = the company has a model but it has not been validated
    5 = the company can consistently generate target customer leads and predict lead conversion rates

- As the company scales the business model, does its economic margin increase year-to-year? (gross margin, operating margin and EBITDA)

    0 = no increase
    1 = slight increase
    3 = moderate increase
    5 = significant increase

Growth Plan: Is the company positioning for exponential growth?

A: Marquee Customers: Are the company's key customers lighthouse references?

- Is the company building strong relationships with marquee customers

    0 = no
    1 = have plans to do it
    3 = have a formal program and have started the process
    5 = have 5 or more strategic partnerships

- Are marquee customers involved in product innovation, testing and validation?

    0 = no
    1 = have developed a plan to involve them
    3 = are somewhat involved according to the plan
    5 = are involved consistently

- Are the key customers responsible for a substantial portion of new leads?

    0 = current customers
    1 = current customers are not making referrals
    3 = current customers are making referrals
    5 = current customers are making regular referrals and actively championing our products/services

B. Alliances and Sales Distribution Channels: Is the company leveraging growth through alliances and non-direct sales/marketing channels?

- Is the company leveraging credible industry alliances for growth or added capability? (Generating revenue with the company or filing in a capability gap of the company – co-marketing, private label)

    0 = no plans in place
    1 = would like to but only have plans in place
    3 = started to, but not producing any results yet
    5 = yes, and the company is seeing results

- Are the company's indirect sales distribution channels developed and working (partners are actively selling your products for you)?

    0 = no
    1 = starting to develop sales channels
    3 = channels are in place but not producing desired results
    5 = channels are in place and revenue from the channels is increasing

C: External – Merger/Acquisition (does the company supplement internal growth with external acquisition plans?)

- Has the company defined a potential acquisition strategy (accretive, economical, profitable?)

    0 = not defined
    1 = thought about it
    3 = defined and documented
    5 = defined, documented, approved, with a pipeline of targets

- Is the company executing the strategy at a rate that would double the company's revenues in the next two years?

    0 = not executing
    1 = executing- adding incremental revenues
    3 = executing and on track to grow revenues by 50% over a two-year period
    5 = yes

- Does the company have a proven integration model?

    0 = haven't thought about it
    1 = don't try to force integration and let it happen naturally
    3 = have to develop a plan on a one-off basis for each acquisition
    5 = has a proven, repeatable process that includes products, customers and support systems (IT, Finance, HR, Admin) integrated within a specific timeframe

Execution Results: What's the bottom line?

- Revenue growth can scale to $50m/100m/$250 m, and is consistent with past trends, within three years? (Currently $10m then grows to $50m, currently $50m then grows to $100m, and currently $100m then grows to $250m)

    0 = can't get there
    1 = don't know if revenues can scale that fast
    3 = can scale but will take longer than 3 years with the current plan
    5 = can scale that fast and are on track to do it

- Annual revenue growth rate is greater than 50%?

    0 = no growth rate
    1 = <10% growth
    3 = 20% growth
    5 = 50% growth

- The company follows a budget and operation plan and trends show successful execution

    0 = no
    1 = have a plan but aren't following it
    3 = have a plan, are falling short, but are making changes
    5 = yes, and the company has hit and plans to hit projection targets

- Current operations are cash flow positive?

    0 = no, and more than four-quarters out
    1 = no, but will within 1 year
    3 = no, but will within 2 quarters
    5 = yes, and sustainable

- The company's gross margin and operating margins are positive and increasing?

    0 = not increasing
    1 = erratic/variable increase/decrease
    3 = they are staying the same – remaining constant
    5 = increasing above comparable averages

- The company is retaining existing customers (positive trends in customer retention)?

    0 = don't know or losing customers
    1 = losing customers but have a plan to address the problem
    3 = retaining current customers
    5 = retaining current customers and increasing/upselling business with them

- The company has established a strong economic barrier to entry?

    0 = no barrier
    1 = probably are some barriers but haven't made any plans to take advantage or create advantage
    3 = credible plans to do so before competitors
    5 = the company has established one or more economic barriers which currently places a permanent (or significant) disadvantage to competitors

Board of Directors & Essential Experts: Is the board a leverage point for expanding growth?

- Majority of board members are independent directors?

    0 = no independent directors
    1 = 25% independent directors
    3 = 50% independent directors
    5 – 80% independent directors

- There is a separation of roles/duties between board members and management?

    0 = none
    1 = some separate roles
    3 = mostly separate roles
    5 = completely separate roles

- Members of the board have previous public board experience?

    0 = none
    1 = 20% have public experience
    3 = 40% have public experience
    5 = 60% have public experience

- Are the board members executives, >5% shareholders and understand and are aligned with strategies, vision and direction?

    0 = no alignment – everyone has different opinions
    1 = understand
    3 = understand and aligned
    5 = understand, aligned and fully supportive

- There is a mix of industry, business and functional expertise on the board?

    0 = no mix
    1 = slight mix/balance
    3 = moderate mix/balance
    5 = strong mix/balance

Management & Organization: Does the company have an inside-out management team?

- The company has clear roles articulated for CEO (external with customers, investors, partners) and COO (process, operations, product execution).

    0 = no role definitions
    1 = same person for both roles
    3 = two people but roles not well-defined
    5 = clear roles established and working

- Is an experienced senior management team complete?

    0 = no management team in place, the board is running the company
    1 = needs a CEO or CFO
    3 = has a strong CEO and CFO but needs remaining executives (marketing, operations, sales)
    5 = has a complete proven management team

- Does management have public company experience?

    0 = none
    1 = 1-2 years (CEO, CFO each)
    3 = 2-5 years (CEO, CFO each)
    5 = 5+ years (CEO, CFO each)

- Has the management team had significant past successes?

    0 = none
    1 = some success
    3 = moderate success
    5 = significant success

- The management team understands the 1-2 initiatives that will leverage their growth ten-fold

    0 = no
    1 = can't articulate the initiatives
    3 = can articulate the initiatives but haven't executed them
    5 = can articulate and are executing the initiatives

- Has the company aligned organization structure, roles, processes, and accountability measures?

    0 = no
    1 = has an organization chart
    3 = has an organization chart, processes and information flows and goals
    5 = yes, and are consistently measuring the progress/success and are holding people accountable (reviews, bonus plans, compensation)

Compliance & Governance: Is the company currently compliant?

- Is the company compliant in its reporting status?

    0 = no
    1 = has plans to do so
    3 = haven't been but will be in one quarter
    5 = yes

- Is the company Sarbanes-Oxley compliant?

    0 = no
    1 = partially
    3 = will be in 2 quarters
    5 = yes

- Are Board committees functioning effectively? (audit, compliance, compensation?)

    0 = no
    1 = have no committees
    3 = have an independent committee chairman established
    5 = yes, meeting regularly as independent committees and meeting reporting requirements

- Are qualified external advisors in place? (legal, accounting, audit)

    0 = no
    1 = use advisors inconsistently or advisors don't have public company experience
    3 = advisors have a moderate amount of public company experience
    5 = advisors have greater than 10 public companies as clients

Equity and Debt Profile:

- Equity, debt and preferred covenants allow flexibility for funding and expansion over the next three years?

    0 = no
    1 = onerous covenants and significant restructuring required (reverse split, lock-ups, tails etc.)
    3 = onerous covenants but holders are willing to work with new funding
    5 = present debt and equity covenants do not prohibit or inhibit future funding capability

- The management team participates in an equity plan, which allows for their ownership to be > 20% of fully diluted equity.

    0 = management doesn't have any equity
    1 = less than 5%
    3 = between 10-15%
    5 = 20% but less than 49%

- Current equity profile allows for a share price >$5.00 per share within 2 years based on projected growth and industry comparables

    0 = no
    1 = no, it would take significant restructuring
    3 = yes, but there isn't any margin for missing the plan
    5 = yes, and the stock price can reach $5.00 per share without any restructuring

Investor Relations Strategy:

The financing plan is aligned with the growth strategy?

    0 = no plan
    1 = started to raise money when we didn't have any
    3 = financing is planned and being executed but has had limited success
    5 = financing is planned, is being executed and is progressing

- Will new funds help create a significant milestone or tipping point?

    0 = funds will be used to reduce liabilities
    1 = will significantly strengthen the balance sheet
    3 = will be used for developing a new market or a new product launch (not R&D)
    5 = new funds will be used for an acquisition or to accelerate the proven growth model

- Has the company completed a meaningful professional investor round?

    0 = no
    1 = tried but failed
    3 = less than $1 million raised
    5 = greater than $2 million raised

- Investor relations and public relations strategies are developed

    0 = no investor or public relations programs are in place
    1 = IR/PR programs are initiated
    3 = functioning IR + PR programs
    5 = a recognized IR/PR firm, internal IR/PR activities, resulting in increased trading volume & ownership

• Is the company sourcing the right investors to match the company's current stage/profile and growth direction?

   0 = don't know who should be targeted
   1 = have identified target investors, but not contacted them
   3 = relationships are established with targeted investors
   5 = targets are acquiring stock and increasing their positions with the company

• Float > 50% of the outstanding shares?

   0 = less than 10%
   1 = 10 - 15%
   3 = 25 - 40 %
   5 = > 50%

• Monthly trading volume > 20% of float?

   0 = less than 1%
   1 = 1-5%
   3 = 10 -15%
   5 = > 20%

   Your Total: _____

Tally the individual score. Then compare them. Quite likely you'll have new eye-opening insights and possibly a new picture of how aligned each of your executives and board are – or not.

Whatever the answers, they will certainly trigger some lively discussions and set the stage for getting better prepped for new investors and future fundraising.

(Im)Proving Your Pitch

I've reviewed, edited, written, and tweaked more Pitch Decks than I can count: 3,000 or so would likely be a low estimate, between reading those of potential clients, as well as keeping others up-to-date. Many of these decks poorly represent what might be a great offer of a company, person, product, or service – because the messaging is all wrong and it misses essential marks.

Your "pitching" job as a leader is still as straightforward as A B C (always be closing.) However, how that pitch is best accomplished these days has changed a bit. For any successful sale -- be it of yourself, your brand, your services, or your company -- to any 'investor' -- financial, employer, partner, customer, or community -- you must demonstrate a deep understanding of a problem they can relate to because here lies your value. You need to show that you grasp their pain, understand the costs, and see what's not working. This understanding is the key to making an investor (= the buyer of anything) feel seen, heard and understood.

Once you've established your understanding of the problem, the next step is to create a sense of urgency. If you've convincingly explained why you, your company, and/or product/services are the inevitable choice, you need to prompt the question, 'Why are you waiting?' This will make your audience feel the need to act now, as you clarify how the waiting only adds to the pain and costs of what's not working.

Then, you need to define a straightforward use of their investment. If you're a company seeking investors -- clearly define exactly how the funds invested will be used. If you're selling yourself or a service -- clearly state your intentions and what you will deliver. If you're selling a product -- clearly state what your product will do and the resulting benefits.

Lastly, it's crucial to prove and substantiate that you've executed before and are still doing it now. This will instill confidence in your "investor" about your abilities and make them feel reassured about their potential investment. This could be in the form of references and referrals.

If you genuinely believe in your "offer" you have every right to sell it by creating a real sense of FOMO -- that "fear of missing out." FOMO is a powerful psychological trigger that can be used to create urgency and drive action. Everything you say and do should serve to others as a reminder of either: I wish I did, or better, I'm glad I did. In other words, make every "investor" of whatever you're selling think: "I'll regret this later if I don't invest now."

If you're working on a presentation – get this messaging delivered in 15 pages or less – and you'll be well into starting an investor relationship. Remember – "The real opportunity for securing investment starts the moment an investor begins to engage with questions." So next up, let's look at just how deep those questions can go!

Into the Depths of Due Diligence

Now, let's examine the questions that you will inevitably be asked. These are the questions that probe into the heart of your business strategy, your ability to execute, and your readiness for the challenges ahead.

Grab a notebook or your computer and prepare to start making notes. If you don't readily know the answers to these questions, you will need to start gathering information and filling in the blanks. The more of these questions that you can thoroughly answer now, the smoother any conversation with a banking partner or investor will be in the future.

Company Overview

What is the company's legal structure (LLC, corporation, etc.)?

In what industry does the company operate, and what is its competitive positioning within this industry?

What is the company's mission, vision, and core values?

How long has the company been in operation?

Who are the company's founders and current executives? What are their professional backgrounds and track records?

What is the company's geographic footprint, and are there plans for international expansion?

What recent milestones or achievements can demonstrate momentum (e.g., partnerships, awards)?

What is the company's brand reputation in its industry or among customers

Prepare a SWOT analysis (Strengths, Weaknesses, Opportunities, Threats) to summarize the company's positioning.

Prior Investor History and Capitalization

Capitalization Table (Cap Table):

What is the current ownership structure, and what percentage do founders, employees, and external investors hold?

Provide a detailed and up-to-date capitalization table, including all equity holders, percentage ownership, and type of equity (common, preferred, etc.)

Are there any existing equity or debt agreements that could impact an IPO or funding?

Are there any outstanding convertible securities, warrants, or options? If so, what are their terms and conversion mechanics?

Have any shares been reserved for an employee stock option plan (ESOP) or future issuances?

Friends and Family Rounds:

Have you conducted any friends and family funding rounds? If so:

How much capital was raised, and on what terms?

Are there any informal agreements or obligations (e.g., preferential returns)?

Are there any active relationships or expectations from early investors that could impact the IPO process?

Venture Capital (VC) Investors:

Have you received funding from venture capital or private equity investors? If so:

Who are the key investors, and what is their stake in the company?

Are there any liquidation preferences, anti-dilution clauses, or other rights associated with their investments?

Do any VC investors hold board seats, and how active are they in company operations?

Are there any veto rights, drag-along, or tag-along provisions in your investor agreements that could affect the IPO?

Previous Investment Banking Relationships:

Have you worked with investment banks or financial advisors in the past? If so:

What services were provided (e.g., M&A, capital raising)?

Were there any success fees, retainers, or other financial arrangements?

Are there any ongoing agreements or "tails" (e.g., rights to fees on subsequent capital raises)?

Were there any syndicate partners or co-lead banks involved in previous financing efforts?

Debt and Equity Dynamics:

Are there any outstanding debts or bridge loans that include equity components or conversion options?

Has the company previously engaged in mezzanine financing or hybrid instruments?

Have any investors been promised special terms that could impact the IPO process (e.g., board representation, pre-emptive rights)?

Investor Relations and Agreements:

Does the company have an investor relations strategy in place?

Have any investors expressed concerns or dissent regarding the company's decisions in any particular areas?

Are there side agreements with specific investors (e.g., preferred treatment, voting agreements)?

What is the company's strategy for transitioning existing investors (e.g., lock-up agreements post-IPO)?

How does the company plan to engage with institutional investors versus retail investors?

How does the company currently manage market expectations, earnings guidance, etc.?

Tail Relationships and Obligations:

Are there any "tail" clauses in contracts with prior investment banks, advisors, or brokers – or any other service provider -- that could require payment upon a successful IPO or subsequent fundraising event?

Have you reviewed these contracts with legal counsel to ensure no unexpected claims arise during the IPO process?

Business Model and Strategy

What is the company's primary business model (B2B, B2C, etc.)?

What are the main revenue streams, and what percentage of revenue does each contribute?

What is the company's growth strategy (e.g., market expansion, product diversification, M&A)?

Who are the company's key customers, and how concentrated is the customer base?

What are the customer acquisition costs (CAC) and lifetime value (LTV)?

How does the company retain customers, and what are its churn rates?

What metrics does the company use to measure success (e.g., KPIs)

Dive into unit economics and scalability potential. Include specific strategic partnerships or alliances that could enhance growth.

Financial Performance

What are the company's historical financial results (revenue, gross profit, EBITDA, net income) over the past 3-5 years?

What is the company's current financial health (debt levels, cash reserves, working capital)?

What are the company's gross and net profit margins, and how do they compare to industry benchmarks?

Has the company conducted any financial audits? If so, by which firm(s)?

What are the company's current financial projections for the next 3-5 years?

How is revenue distributed across geographies, products, or services?

Are there any non-recurring or extraordinary items in historical financials?

Scenario analysis (best, base, and worst-case financial forecasts). Assess sensitivity to economic downturns or market shifts.

Market Opportunity

What is the size and growth rate of the company's target market(s)?

What market trends and dynamics could positively or negatively impact the company?

Who are the company's primary competitors, and what differentiates the company from them?

Does the company have a defensible market position or unique selling proposition (e.g., intellectual property, brand strength)?

What barriers to entry exist in the company's market?

What is the Total Addressable Market (TAM), Serviceable Addressable Market (SAM), and Serviceable Obtainable Market (SOM)?

How has the market evolved in the last five years, and what is the expected trajectory? (increasing, declining, etc.)

Competitor benchmarking data (market share, pricing strategy, customer satisfaction).

Products and Services

What are the company's primary products or services, and what is their lifecycle stage (e.g., emerging, mature)?

Are there any flagship products or services that contribute significantly to revenue?

What is the company's product development pipeline or innovation strategy?

How does the company protect its intellectual property (e.g., patents, trademarks)

What is the customer feedback or satisfaction rate for each product/service?

Are there any dependencies on third-party vendors for product delivery?

What is the company's strategy for phasing out underperforming products?

Any environmental, social, and governance (ESG) compliance or sustainability issues/initiatives.

Operational Readiness

What is the company's current operational capacity, and how scalable is it?

What supply chain risks or dependencies exist?

Does the company have the necessary infrastructure to support rapid growth?

What investments are needed to support future growth (e.g., technology, facilities)?

What is the average utilization rate of the company's production capacity?

How does the company ensure operational efficiency and mitigate bottlenecks?

What disaster recovery or business continuity plans are in place?

Review assessments of digital transformation, automation, or other technologies that enhance efficiency.

Governance and Leadership

What is the composition and experience of the company's board of directors?

How strong is the company's executive team in terms of operational and financial expertise?

Does the company have a clear corporate governance structure in place?

Are there any significant key person dependencies? Are insurances in place?

What diversity initiatives does the company promote within leadership and the board?

Are there independent directors, and how do they contribute to governance?

What are the succession plans for key executives?

Ask for the board's structure and whether they follow recognized corporate governance frameworks (e.g., Sarbanes-Oxley compliance).

Legal and Regulatory Compliance

Are there any ongoing or past legal disputes involving the company?

Is the company in compliance with all industry-specific regulations?

Does the company have adequate risk management practices in place?

Are there any legal or regulatory hurdles to going public?

Are there any pending patents or intellectual property disputes?

How does the company monitor and adapt to changes in regulations?

Has the company conducted a legal audit recently? If so, what were the findings?

Include a section on cybersecurity and data privacy compliance that is in place.

Readiness for Public Offering

What are the primary objectives for going public (e.g., raising capital, brand visibility, shareholder liquidity, funding growth, funding research and development, marketing)?

What are the anticipated uses of funds raised through an IPO?

Does the company have a clear value proposition for potential investors?

How well does the company's financial reporting and forecasting align with public company standards?

Has the company conducted a pre-IPO valuation or received feedback from potential underwriters?

What steps has the company taken to ensure compliance with SEC regulations?

What is the proposed IPO pricing strategy?

Engagements with any financial, legal, and operational advisors for funding readiness.

Risks and Challenges

What are the primary risks the company faces (e.g., market, operational, competitive)?

How has the company historically managed risks and uncertainties?

What external factors could significantly impact the company post-IPO?

What internal controls or risk management systems does the company have in place?

How does the company manage currency, geopolitical or supply chain risks?

What are the specific risks associated with becoming a public company (e.g., increased transparency, shareholder activism)?

Prepare a risk heat map highlighting critical risks by likelihood and impact.

Post-IPO Plans

How will the company ensure compliance with public company reporting and governance requirements?

What strategies will be in place to attract and maintain investor interest?

What is the long-term vision for the company as a publicly traded entity?

What is the company's strategy for share buybacks or equity issuance in the future?

How will the company manage public relations and media coverage post-IPO?

What benchmarks will the company use to evaluate IPO success?

Prepare post-IPO/funding metrics for measuring stock performance, such as stock liquidity, analyst coverage, and institutional ownership percentages.

Whether you already have this information organized in a comprehensive business plan or due diligence package, or if it's scattered and in need of updating, here's the bottom line: Every question outlined in this chapter reflects the critical information you'll be expected to provide as a CEO seeking investors to bring your vision to life. This information is crucial for your success.

Staying prepared and keeping this information current isn't just a one-time task; it's an ongoing responsibility that will make you more effective, confident and agile in leading your company. Having these details at your fingertips will streamline investor discussions and empower you to focus on achieving your long-term goals. Trust me, assembling and maintaining this information will transform your day-to-day work from reactive to proactive, making your role as CEO infinitely more manageable and impactful, while reducing the stress of the unknown.

Chapter 6

Capital Allocation and The Leadership Role in Maintaining Financial Health & Sustainable Growth

As a CEO, you are more than just a decision-maker -- you're a steward of your company's future. Few responsibilities highlight this more clearly than the art of capital allocation. The strategic foresight required for this balancing act underpins everything: growth, innovation, shareholder trust and resilience. It's not just about numbers; it's about shaping a vision for your company and ensuring that every dollar supports the present and the future.

Capital allocation is about making choices that resonate far beyond the boardroom. It's about asking, "Where will this decision take us?" -- and balancing bold innovation with steady, sustainable growth. Whether investing in cutting-edge research, raising equity or taking on debt, stock buy backs, rewarding loyal shareholders with dividends, or pursuing strategic acquisitions, every choice carries weight. The challenge is to keep your footing, even as the stakes rise.

Let's explore how capital allocation becomes a process and a tool for transformational leadership, inspiring you to make strategic decisions that can shape the future of your company.

Capital Allocation: Shaping the Future, One Decision at a Time

Capital allocation isn't just a task on your to-do list -- it's the engine that powers your company's evolution. It signals what matters most: innovation, shareholder returns, or strategic expansion. Done well, it builds trust, positions your company for resilience, and keeps your vision alive in an ever-changing market.

This isn't about throwing money at opportunities; it's about aligning resources with long-term goals while staying agile enough to pivot when needed. It's where strategy meets execution and where great leaders prove their mettle.

Balancing Investments in Research & Development

Research and Development (R&D) is the soul of innovation. It's where ideas become breakthroughs, and possibilities turn into competitive advantages. But let's be honest: R&D isn't for the faint of heart. It requires patience, courage, and the willingness to invest in what might not pay off -- at least not immediately.

As a CEO, your role in R&D goes beyond approving budgets. It includes essential considerations such as:

Setting Priorities That Matter: Where should your R&D dollars go? Which projects align with your vision and the market's emerging needs? Focus creates impact.

Balancing Boldness with Practicality: High-risk innovations are exciting, but incremental improvements can sustain your company's edge. A mix of both keeps your portfolio dynamic.

Tracking and Adapting: R&D is a journey. Monitoring progress, staying informed, and pivoting if something isn't working are essential leadership skills.

When you commit to meaningful R&D, you signal to your team and stakeholders that you're in it for the long haul -- that your company is here to lead, not just follow.

Raising Equity or Taking on Debt

Pretty much every Company leader with grand visions arrives at that big day when friends and family money along with that of venture capitalists all point to the next level: It's time to partner with an investment bank so the Company can get knowledgeable strategic advice necessary from an advisory team who will help them prepare for a successful capital raise from quality investors; possibly IPO, reverse merge, up-list or move to one of the stock market exchanges; and, ultimately navigate the capital markets in the aftermath.

Whether for an initial public offering (IPO) or other financial reasons, choosing the right investment bank and institutional funds are cornerstones of any successful capital-raising and long-term-corporate health strategy. Aligning with quality and qualified financial partners best ensures access to the necessary capital, while positioning your company for long-term growth and success in the market. The wrong choice (while often popular) can and will destroy your Company and vision in unimaginable ways. Be assured: I've seen it and I'm not kidding.

So, how do you identify suitable partners? What are the criteria for selecting investment banks and funds? And, how can you determine the optimal timing for raising money? Let's break it down.

Identifying and Aligning with the Right Investment Bank

Investment bankers and their associated team members are critical partners responsible for connecting your company with the capital markets, creating all kinds of financial and strategic introductions, structuring deals, and providing knowledgeable advice. When selecting an investment bank, smart CEOs consider the following factors:

Industry Expertise: Look for banks with a strong track record in your sector. They will likely have better relationships with relevant investors and a deeper understanding of industry-specific challenges and opportunities.

Reputation and Credibility: Choose a bank with a solid reputation and a proven history of successful capital raises. Investors often place trust in deals backed by reputable institutions.

Deal Size Fit: This one is so important! Ensure the bank typically handles deals of your size. Larger banks may prioritize bigger clients, while boutique firms may offer more personalized attention for smaller or mid-sized raises.

Consider the Source: Where's the money coming from? Does the firm have a strong retail capability or will the money you need come from just a few large funds? This is a crucial consideration for the long-term health of your Company as it can impact trading volume and volatility. Also, what is the "hold history" of those funds? Quick money can be quite painful; especially so if you're not fully aware of what kind of relationship you're getting into.

Geographic Reach: Depending on your company's focus, selecting a bank with strong regional or international connections to tap into the most relevant investor base might be immensely valuable. Ask these questions!

Advisory Strength: The bank should demonstrate strategic insights beyond securing capital, offering valuable advice on timing, structuring, up listings, investor relations, strategic partnerships and market positioning. The broader the core experience of the banking team, the greater potential for your success assuming all factors above are also considered.

Partnering with Funds That Align with Your Vision

When seeking institutional investors, aligning with the right funds is equally important as choosing the right investment banking partner. Institutional investors can bring more than just capital -- they can provide strategic guidance, network access and market credibility. Consider these factors when you're meeting with fund managers:

Investment Mandate: Target funds whose investment criteria align with your company's stage of growth, sector and geographic focus. Otherwise? You're wasting precious time. Don't try to "change their mind" because "if they only understood how wonderful your company is…" This is not how the game works. Appreciate the "No's." And, don't forget to ask them, "What would it take to get to 'Yes'?"

Track Record: Review the fund's history of investments, including its ability to support portfolio companies through growth stages and exits. Ask about their hold time. Are they flippers? In and out of the stock the minute the lock-up ends? Don't be embarrassed to ask. They might not tell you – but you'll regret not asking… even if the answer isn't exactly true.

Value-Add Capabilities: Identify fund managers that can contribute beyond financing, such as offering expertise or connections to other stakeholders. These connections can be priceless.

Cultural Fit: Assess whether the fund's values and approach to governance align with your company's culture and long-term goals. This is a biggy. Again, I'll say: Ignore this at your own peril.

When to Raise Capital

Timing is critical when raising funds, as it can significantly impact your company's valuation, investor interest, and strategic outcomes.

Consider each of the following factors:

Business Milestones: Raise funds when you have achieved or are on the verge of reaching significant milestones, such as product development, key partnerships, or market expansion, as these can enhance your valuation.

Market Conditions: Assess the broader economic and market climate. Strong equity markets, low-interest-rate environments, or sector-specific growth trends may provide favorable capital-raising conditions.

Runway Requirements: Plan funding rounds well before running out of cash. Ideally, begin fundraising at least 6–12 months before you need additional capital to maintain operations and growth initiatives. Desperation is rarely accompanied by the best terms for your Company and its existing Shareholders. Perceptively smart CEOs plan and initiate fund raising when they have plenty of cash in the bank.

Strategic Growth Opportunities: If a compelling growth opportunity arises, such as an acquisition or entering a new market, raising funds proactively can enable you to seize the moment.

Cost of Capital: Consider the cost of equity versus debt financing and aim to raise funds when terms are favorable and dilution is minimal.

Aligning with the right investment bank and investors, along with identifying the best timing for your capital raise, are essential to effectively achieve your company's strategic goals. By selecting partners that share your vision while leveraging market opportunities, you can secure the financial resources needed to fuel growth, navigate challenges and build shareholder value.

It's crucial to regularly reassess your capital strategy to ensure it aligns with your company's evolving objectives and market dynamics. This kind of "stress test," focused on regular capital-needs reassessments, will make you feel and look both vigilant and proactive in the eyes of shareholders – while also showcasing your competency in managing your company's financial resources.

Stock Buy Backs

If ever flush with a lot of cash in the coffers – a CEO fantasy dream – either the CEO, CFO or the board may suggest that the Company strategically initiates a stock buyback (or a share repurchase) for several reasons which are often tied to its financial health, market conditions, or long-term objectives. Sometimes the reason is to signal confidence in the company's financial stability and future growth prospects. Whatever the reason by repurchasing shares, the company demonstrates that it believes its stock is undervalued, which can boost investor confidence and drive up the stock price. Additionally, reducing the number of shares outstanding increases earnings per share (EPS), as profits are spread over a smaller base, making the company appear more profitable on a per-share basis.

Another motivation for a stock buyback is to optimize the company's capital structure. When a firm has excess cash or access to low-cost debt, buying back shares can be a more attractive use of funds than investing in uncertain projects or holding cash that generates minimal returns. It can also be a way to return value to shareholders without committing to ongoing dividend payments, offering flexibility in capital allocation. Certainly, share repurchases play a crucial role in enhancing shareholder value, possibly helping to offset the dilutive effects of employee stock options and other equity compensation plans, while also maintaining the value of existing shareholders' stakes. Overall, stock buybacks can enhance shareholder value, signal financial health, and align the company's capital strategy with its broader goals.

All that said – not all investors love seeing stock buy backs as a financial cash allocation strategy. This is where CEOs need to have their leadership messaging on point. Otherwise, the market will wonder: Why the heck isn't this company using the money on hand to innovate, pay a dividend or use it in some way to grow? Which…brings us to the idea of those dividends.

Dividends: Strengthening Shareholder Trust

The possibility of declaring a dividend(s) is another dream many CEOs will only fantasize about. More than payouts – dividends are statements. They say, "We value you and are here for the long term." But dividends also come with trade-offs, pulling resources away from reinvestment opportunities.

Here's how you approach them wisely:

Find the Balance: Satisfying shareholders is essential, as is reinvesting for growth. Striking the right mix is critical.

Build Stability: A predictable, sustainable dividend policy fosters confidence, even during times of economic turbulence.

Explore Alternatives: Sometimes, share buybacks offer a smarter path to shareholder value. The choice depends on your strategy and your market position.

Dividends are a tool, but they're also a promise. They can strengthen trust and reinforce your company's financial health when managed thoughtfully.

Acquisitions: Expanding with Purpose

Having done all kinds of investor polling over the past 30+ years, here's an interesting observation: CEOs always think "the market" will love that they're doing an acquisition. Shareholders and the overall "Market" often have very differing opinions on the value of the acquisition, namely, whether it was a good idea…or not. That question is often followed by a big: "But why?" Further, acquisition announcements are the surest way to trigger divisive online chat about past performance by the management team: Namely, whether leadership was doing well-enough with what they had on their plates already – and, therefore, whether they are prepared, ready and capable to add more to the mix. Lots of digesting conversations and research before an acquisition is essential as is making sure management's rationale is understood. All of this is paramount to maintaining and ideally even gaining shareholder support.

Acquisitions are often perceived by management teams, boards and sometimes their significant shareholders as the fast lane to growth -- but they are not without risks. And it is those risks that often make the market question a CEO's acquisition decisions. This is because a successful acquisition requires more than financial resources: It demands a financial wherewithal; strategic fit; cultural alignment; and, a clear understanding of how it enhances your company's trajectory.

As a CEO, your role is to:

Seek Synergy: Look for opportunities that complement your company's strengths and fill gaps you couldn't address, as readily, and organically.

Do Your Homework: Due diligence isn't optional -- it's essential. Assemble and work closely with a team that has the talent and experience to dig deeply to uncover risks and ensure the acquisition aligns with your vision.

Don't Be Afraid to Change Your Mind: If at any point during your due diligence you begin to doubt the transaction – don't be afraid to renegotiate or walk away from the transaction. Sometimes this is the wisest option. It's like that old saying: Even if you put lipstick on a pig if it's a pig, it is now just a pig with lipstick.

Lead Integration: The real work begins after any acquisition. Bringing teams together to foster collaboration is essential. Aligning cultures to unlock the acquisition's potential is not easy – and then there are all the other logistics – like merging technology platforms and more.

When done right, acquisitions don't just add -- they amplify, creating value that resonates across your organization and beyond. Done wrong, they can crush shareholder support and trust.

Certainly, there's more to discuss with acquisitions – but those are conversations best had with a quality banking team of advisors. These brief thoughts are merely an introductory teaser.

A Framework for Strategic Balancing

Let's wrap this section up with a few final thoughts for your contemplative pleasure.

Capital allocation is never one-size-fits-all. It's a dynamic process that requires foresight, adaptability and a deep connection to your company's mission. Here's how to keep it balanced:

Think Long-Term: Focus on sustainable success, not just quarterly wins. Every decision should reflect your commitment to enduring growth.

Stay Flexible: Markets shift, challenges arise, and new opportunities emerge. Build adaptability into your strategy to stay ahead of the curve.

Communicate Transparently: Shareholders and stakeholders want to understand your decisions. Be open, clear and consistent about how your choices align with your vision. This transparency builds trust and understanding, both are key elements in successful capital allocation.

Leading with Purpose and Precision

As a CEO, your choices ripple through your organization and beyond. Capital allocation isn't just about spreadsheets -- it's about shaping a future that reflects your company's values and potential.

When you balance financial health with sustainable growth, you're not just managing a company but inspiring it. You're proving that profitability and purpose can coexist, creating value for shareholders, opportunities for employees, and a lasting legacy.

At the end of the day, leadership for perceptive leaders is about more than decisions -- it's about their collective impact. And through thoughtful, strategic capital allocation, you have the power to build something extraordinary.

Chapter 7

Crafting and Sustaining Equity and Debt Strategies for Optimal Financial Health

As a CEO or CFO, your role transcends operational leadership -- you are the architect of your company's financial future. In the dynamic landscape of leading a publicly traded company, equity and debt strategies serve as more than just financial instruments; they are the cornerstone of growth, resilience and opportunity.

The ability to strategically balance these two pillars demands foresight, adaptability, and an unwavering focus on your company's long-term goals. When approached thoughtfully, equity and debt are not mere obligations but powerful opportunities to amplify your company's potential.

While we addressed financial stewardship and cash allocation in the last chapter, here we're going to go a bit deeper into leveraging equity and debt to align financial health with corporate purpose. By selecting an investment banking partner and an advisory team that truly understands your vision while being fully committed to helping you achieve it, you can confidently navigate every growth stage with clarity and optimism for the future.

The Foundations of Equity and Debt Strategy

Equity and debt are the twin engines of corporate finance, each with unique benefits and challenges. A balanced approach ensures that your Company can scale, innovate and remain agile in changing market conditions.

Equity and Debt strategies are different – though, with the right investment bank advisory team and the right investors, you'll be able to identify, merge and establish ways each can contribute significantly while factoring in the ultimate market perception of the transaction.

Considerations for each include:

Equity Strategy Considerations:

- **Manage Dilution Thoughtfully:** Every equity raise affects ownership. Maintaining investor confidence means balancing immediate needs with long-term trust. Dilution, the reduction in the ownership percentage of each shareholder, caused by the issuance of new shares, is a key consideration in equity strategy.
- **Time the Market Strategically:** Raising equity during favorable conditions maximizes valuation and minimizes Dilution -- timing is everything.
- **Align Decisions with Shareholders:** Share issuances, buybacks or dividends should reflect your broader strategy and resonate with shareholder expectations.

Debt Strategy Considerations:

- **Optimize Cost of Debt:** Debt can be a cost-effective way to fuel growth, especially when interest rates are low, *but* managing repayment obligations is critical.
- **Monitor Leverage Ratios:** Healthy debt-to-equity and interest coverage ratios are essential to maintaining financial stability and market confidence.

- **Structure Maturities Wisely:** Stagger debt maturities to preserve liquidity and flexibility while avoiding repayment bottlenecks.

When integrated thoughtfully, these funding strategies provide the financial foundation your company needs to thrive regardless of market conditions. The key here? Get good advice and heed it accordingly, ahead of making any funding decisions.

Strategic Use of Equity and Debt Across Growth Stages

Every stage of growth presents unique challenges -- and opportunities. Your approach to equity and debt should evolve alongside your company's journey. Let's look at a variety of "growing pains" faced by companies.

Early Growth Stage:

The Focus: Fueling rapid expansion and capturing market share.

- **Equity:** Prioritize equity financing to reduce the burden of fixed payments and attract investors who believe in your vision.
- **Debt:** Use sparingly, focusing on low-risk, short-term options like working capital loans or grants.

Scaling and Expansion Stage:

The Focus: Investing in operations, innovation and new markets.

- **Equity:** Leverage strong stock performance to raise funds through secondary offerings or convertible securities.
- **Debt:** Increase leverage prudently for capital expenditures or acquisitions, locking favorable long-term rates.

Maturity Stage:
The Focus: Stabilizing and maximizing shareholder value.

- **Equity:** Implement share buybacks to reward shareholders and support the stock price alongside consistent dividends.
- **Debt:** Use established cash flows to optimize the capital structure, funding strategic initiatives without overextending.

Turnaround or Distressed Stage:

The Focus: Preserving liquidity and rebuilding stability.

- **Equity:** Issue equity cautiously to avoid signaling distress while seeking strategic partners or private equity support.
- **Debt:** Renegotiate terms, explore restructuring, and focus on stabilizing the balance sheet.

As CEO, along with your CFO and Board of Directors, your ability to balance risk, opportunity, and flexibility at every stage defines your success. Further, the paramount importance of choosing your banking partner carefully cannot be reiterated enough. A good investment banking partner – one that is focused on your company's long-term growth and success -- will help you understand not only the best deal structure at any given point – but also be both knowledgeable and selective as to which funds they introduce to your deal.

Tactics for Optimizing Equity and Debt Strategies

There are a variety of tactics that smart leadership teams apply when determining their equity and debt strategies. These include any or all of the following.

Conduct Regular Capital Structure Reviews:
>Stay ahead by analyzing your company's financial position relative to market conditions, benchmarking against peers, and adjusting as needed.

Build Relationships with Capital Providers:
>Transparency and trust with investors, lenders, and rating agencies facilitate favorable terms and enduring partnerships.

Leverage Market Conditions:
>Capitalize on favorable equity valuations or low interest rates and use hedging instruments to protect against volatility.

Balance Risk and Flexibility:
>Avoid over-leveraging during favorable periods, maintaining liquidity buffers to weather unforeseen challenges.

Align Financing with Strategy:
>Tailor your financing tools to the goals at hand -- use equity for innovation and debt for predictable, revenue-generating investments.

Case Study: Strategic Financing at GiggleTech Solutions.

GiggleTech Solutions, a leading technology company, faced a pivotal moment: It needed to fund ambitious expansion plans while retaining investor confidence in a volatile market.

Initial Situation:
- Equity valuations were high, presenting an ideal fundraising opportunity.
- Rising interest rates posed a challenge for debt financing.

Action Plan:

Equity: A secondary offering raised $50 million, limiting dilution to 8%.

Debt: Existing debt was renegotiated to extend maturities and lock in fixed rates.

Strategic Alignment: Funds were allocated to high-growth projects, with clear ROI projections shared with investors.

Outcome:
GiggleTech's disciplined approach boosted market confidence, resulting in a 25% increase in market capitalization over the 18 months.

Key Takeaways for CEOs and CFOs

- **Stay Proactive:** Review and adapt your capital structure to meet evolving needs and opportunities.
- **Align Financing with Vision:** Every decision should reflect and support your Company's strategic goals. This alignment will keep you focused and purpose-driven, ensuring that every financial move contributes to the realization of your Company's vision.
- **Communicate with Confidence:** Keep stakeholders informed about the rationale behind your strategies, fostering trust and alignment.

The Big Picture

Equity and debt strategies are more than financial tools -- they're the lifelines that keep your Company thriving through every growth stage. The right strategy doesn't just fund your goals; it strengthens your company's resilience, reputation and innovation ability.

As a CEO or CFO, your decisions shape more than just the balance sheet -- they shape the future. Lead with both strategy and heart, embracing your dual role as steward and visionary. In doing so, you'll safeguard your Company's financial health, inspire while building trust, drive innovation, and create lasting value for all stakeholders.

Chapter 8

Balancing Competing Priorities: Quarterly Earnings vs. Long-Term Goals

As a CEO, you navigate a world of continuous trade-offs. On one hand, the pressure to deliver precise, short-term results dominates, driven by quarterly earnings and investor expectations. On the other hand, the allure of long-term vision -- the cornerstone of sustainable growth, innovation, and a lasting legacy -- calls for foresight and strategic patience.

The balancing act between these priorities isn't just a challenge; it's the defining responsibility of modern leadership.

Leading a public company means navigating this tension with perceptiveness, clarity and confidence plus a lot of heart. The goal is not to choose between short vs. long term expectations, but to bring them into alignment under a unified vision, ensuring that today's wins support tomorrow's potential. Let's explore how you, in your executive leadership strategic role, can approach this balance with strategy and even a bit of soul.

Understanding the Tension: Why It Exists

The pressure to deliver short-term results is undeniable. Quarterly earnings represent accountability and transparency, and missing expectations can have immediate consequences.

For starters these may include:

- **Stock Volatility:** Missed earnings often trigger swift market reactions – and not the kind you desire.
- **Reputation at Risk:** A pattern of misses can erode trust in your leadership ability.
- **Activist Investor Scrutiny:** Underperformance may invite activists to seek immediate and often disruptive changes.

But here's the catch: focusing exclusively on the short term can undermine the foundation of long-term success. This happens when companies:

- **Sacrifice Innovation:** Cutting research & development (R&D) or growth initiatives to meet short-term targets.
- **Harm Employee Morale:** Overzealous cost-cutting measures can stagnate talent and motivation.
- **Miss Strategic Opportunities:** Delaying crucial investments to protect immediate financial metrics.

Understanding this dynamic is the first step toward mastering it for your corporate health. So, how do you master it? Let's break it down.

Strategies for Balancing Short-Term and Long-Term Objectives

Striking the right balance between short-term and long-term objectives is a delicate art, yet it is the cornerstone of sustainable success for any Company. While short-term achievements provide the momentum to move forward, it is the long-term vision outlined and fulfilled by the CEO that ensures all efforts are aligned with broader aspirations.

Let's explore practical strategies to harmonize immediate needs with future ambitions, setting the tone with a mindset that embraces adaptability, focus, and purposeful planning.

Establish a Unified Vision
- Create a long-term strategy that inspires confidence and commitment.
- Show how quarterly goals act as milestones to achieve this vision.
- To show progress holistically, highlight metrics beyond earnings -- like customer loyalty, market expansion, or product innovation.

Communicate Transparently with Investors
- Be honest about the trade-offs. Share how near-term actions fuel the long-term strategy.
- Explain decisions clearly -- whether it's increased spending on R&D or restructuring costs -- and connect them to future value.
- Proactively engage long-term investors who prioritize sustainable success over quick wins.

Measure Success with Balanced Metrics
- Combine short- and long-term performance indicators to track progress:
    - **Short-Term:** Revenue, margins, cash flow.
    - **Long-Term:** Brand strength, innovation milestones, market share.
- Keep stakeholders informed with regular updates on both sets of metrics.

Adopt a Dual-Timeline Strategy

- Divide initiatives into distinct horizons:
    - **Horizon 1:** Immediate efficiency and stability.
    - **Horizon 2:** Growth investments in core capabilities.
    - **Horizon 3:** Transformative opportunities like entering new markets or launching groundbreaking technologies.
- Allocate resources strategically to keep all horizons progressing.

Guard Against Short-Termism

- Resist the urge to make hasty cuts or compromises to hit quarterly numbers.
- Educate your board and investors about the risks of short-termism using real-world examples and data.

Engage Employees as Stakeholders

- Connect employees' roles to both short-term wins and the bigger picture.
- Be transparent about decisions affecting budgets, priorities, or growth plans, so your team understands the "why" behind the "what."

Case Study: Bananarama Biotech Inc. Balances Innovation and Earnings

When Bananarama Biotech Inc.'s quarterly burn rate was reported far higher than analysts' projections due to increased R&D spending on an additional clinical trial for a next-generation product, analysts sounded alarms, and the stock price dropped. The CEO faced mounting pressure but stayed resolute.

How the CEO Responded:

1. **Transparent Communication:** During earnings calls, the CEO emphasized how the R&D investment aligned with long-term strategy and innovation goals. He outlined exactly why this additional clinical trial was warranted and how it would be supportive to an ultimate F.D.A. approval and expanded labeling – leading, ultimately upon approval, to greater market share.
2. **Balanced Reporting:** Management began sharing innovation milestones alongside financial metrics, creating a fuller picture of progress.
3. **Media Outreach:** The company shifted its public relations strategy by adding more targeted media outreach. The goal was to secure interviews positioning the leadership team as thought-leaders within their specific sector and as experts in drug development. These articles were then shared with investors in addition to other corporate development announcements. Investors reacted favorably to increasing media coverage, favorable industry positioning, and overall awareness the company was garnering.
4. **Proactive Engagement:** The CEO held detailed discussions with institutional investors, securing their buy-in for the long-term vision.

The Result:

When the new therapeutic was sold to a large pharmaceutical partner, Bananarama Biotech met and exceeded expectations. Investor confidence grew, the stock price rebounded, and the company avoided layoffs or rushed compromises. By staying disciplined and transparent, the CEO demonstrated that long-term thinking delivers.

Best Practices for CEOs

- **Frame Today in the Context of Tomorrow:** Use every opportunity -- earnings calls, board meetings, investor updates -- to show how current results are building toward your future corporate success.

- **Stay the Course:** Consistency inspires confidence. Stick to your strategy, even under pressure.
- **Educate and Inspire Stakeholders:** Help your investors, board and employees understand that short-term sacrifices often lead to long-term gains.

The Big Picture

Balancing quarterly performance with long-term goals isn't an either-or decision -- it's a dynamic dance that requires precision and vision. The most effective CEOs lead with strategy and heart, aligning immediate actions with enduring aspirations.

When you commit to this balance, you're not just delivering results -- you are building trust, fostering resilience and creating a legacy. With clarity, courage and consistency, you can guide your company through the complexities of public leadership, ensuring success today and for years to come.

Chapter 9

Managing Investor Relations: Building Trust and Navigating Activist Investor Pressure

In the high-stakes world of public companies, transparency and accountability are not just ideals -- they are non-negotiable. As the leader of a public company -- or one with plans or on route to becoming public -- you as CEO bear the brunt of accountability with investor relations (IR) acting as your megaphone and shield. Managing IR isn't just about reporting numbers; it's about building trust, fostering relationships, and navigating the challenges of an increasingly vigilant investor base regardless of where your stock trades.

At its best, IR is a cornerstone of leadership, where the art of communication meets the science of strategy. As a CEO, your strategic management of this critical function will shape market perceptions and solidify your company's ability to grow, adapt and thrive -- even under pressure. This is a realm where you hold the reins of messaging, guiding your company's narrative and market perception.

The Role of Investor Relations in Business Strategy

Let's be clear: IR isn't a box you check -- it's a strategic tool that drives credibility and growth.

Think of your IR team as the bridge between your vision and your shareholders' expectations. Investor relations advisors are the storytellers of your company, who connect your mission, strategy and performance to those who have placed their trust -- and money -- in your hands.

Here's why a robust IR strategy is indispensable: it's not just about reacting to market conditions but proactively shaping them. Those you choose as your investor relations advisors are priceless allies who must be chosen carefully as they are "The Face of the Company" when you're otherwise occupied.

As you think through and define a solid investor relations strategy, consider these key points. A good investor relations program should serve as a:

- **Credibility Enhancer:** Transparent, consistent communication builds confidence in your ability to execute your vision.
- **Magnet for Long-Term Investors:** Clear articulation of your strategy attracts institutional investors who value stability over speculation.
- **Market Valuation Ally:** Effective IR reduces volatility by aligning market perceptions with your company's intrinsic value.

Investor relations isn't just a department; IR is a lifeline between leadership and the world beyond your walls. It's a proactive tool, a shield that you can wield to anticipate and address challenges before they become crises.

Building Trust Through Transparent Communication

Trust isn't built in a day but it can surely be lost in a moment. For CEOs, developing an ongoing sense of trust with investors requires honesty, clarity and responsiveness: *not* just during the good times but especially when challenges arise.

Here's how to make trust your most vital asset:

Be Transparent: Investors want the full story, not just the highlight reel. Share successes and setbacks with equal candor. This transparency shows respect for your investors, acknowledging their right to know the complete picture, as repletely as you can disclose it.

Communicate Regularly: Don't let quarterly earnings calls be your only touchpoint. Host investor days, hold one-on-one meetings, and stay visible. And – yes, you are in a regulated industry and you have to be careful that you don't share information that you can't -- BUT -- Do Not Waste Any Analyst or Investor's Time by reading from a script that is verbatim to what they could have read themselves in the earnings release!

Showcase Your Team: Highlight the strength and expertise of your leadership team to reassure investors that your company is in many capable hands. Acknowledge all departments when appropriate.

Articulate Your Vision: Tie your long-term goals to measurable metrics to help investors see and understand the roadmap you've outlined for success.

Under Promise, Over Deliver: Know what you can do. As mentioned above, spell it out. Don't overpromise. Set timelines that you can fulfill. Investors have memories like steel traps. If you miss your deadlines, recognize you are destroying trust. AND, missing deadlines can get very expensive as many private investors will tie penalties to any promises you miss.

Own Your Mistakes: When things go wrong, acknowledge them and outline a plan to address the issue. Investors respect accountability far more than avoidance.

Trust is your currency. Build it wisely, and it will carry you through many triumphs and trials.

Understanding and Mitigating Activist Investor Pressure

Activist investors -- love or dread them -- are part of the game. While more recent media articles are opining that the old-school activist breed is dying, I predict it won't be long before a new batch of activists make their presence known with their respective agendas and demands. At their best, activist investors challenge complacency and bring fresh perspectives. At their worst, they can derail long-term strategies for short-term gains. As a CEO, your role isn't to avoid activists but to engage with them strategically and protect your company's vision.

The Best Proactive Engagement Strategies

Here's a brief high-level summary of the best proactive engagement strategies you'll want to contemplate carefully.

> **Know Your Shareholders:** Understand who owns your stock and their priorities. Knowledge is power.
>
> **Open Dialogue:** Engage early and listen to your shareholders and potential new ones. Many conflicts arise more from misunderstanding than malice.
>
> **Seek Common Ground:** Identify areas of alignment and work toward mutually beneficial solutions.

Strengthen Your Governance and Strategy:

- *Governance Matters*: A strong, independent board shows you're serious about oversight and accountability.
- *Stay Data-Driven*: Your strategic plan should be grounded in compelling, evidence-based insights.

Prepare for Proxy Contests:

- *Scenario Planning*: Anticipate potential challenges and prepare responses in advance.
- *Engage Stakeholders*: Build alliances with long-term investors who understand and support your vision.

Counteract Misinformation:

- *Monitor the Narrative*: Stay attuned to how your company is being discussed in the media and investment circles.
- **Respond Swiftly**: Correct inaccuracies with professionalism and respect -- never with defensiveness.

Activist pressure doesn't have to be a threat. With preparation and engagement, it can become an opportunity for growth.

Case Study: The Turnaround of Widget Whiz Corporation

When Widget Whiz Co., a mid-cap technology firm, faced criticism from activist investor Big Bucks and Beyond Capital (BBC), the stakes were high. BBC labeled the company's R&D investments as wasteful and pushed for divestment of an underperforming division.

How the Widget Whiz CEO Turned It Around:

Engagement: The CEO invited Big Bucks and Beyond Managers for a transparent discussion of concerns. They also offered on-site facility tours.

Strategic Adjustment: After a full review, the division was retained but tied to new performance benchmarks. The CEO worked with the teams, set realistic achievables and presented them in corporate presentations published on its website and via additional public announcements. These became milestone achievements that could be publicly monitored by investors as a scorecard. Ultimately they served to confirm management's decision to be correct.

Proactive Communication: As per above, the Widget Whiz IR team rolled out a detailed plan to all investors, reinforcing the company's long-term vision.

The result? Big Bucks and Beyond withdrew its proxy contest, and Widget Whiz Corporation's stock rose 15% over the year as market confidence rebounded and growth was reported.

Best Practice Lessons for CEOs

- **Stay Ahead:** Regularly evaluate potential vulnerabilities that could attract activist scrutiny.

- **Empower Your Team:** Equip your IR professionals with the tools and authority they need to shine.

- **Foster Relationships:** Build trust with institutional investors -- they'll be your allies in critical moments.

■ *The Big Picture*

Investor relations isn't just about compliance -- it's about connection. It's about showing your stakeholders that you see them, hear them, and respect their role in your Company's journey.

Whether you're building trust through transparency or navigating the complexities of activist pressure, IR is where leadership meets accountability.

At its core, IR is about more than strategy -- it's about stewardship. As a CEO, you have the power to transform challenges into opportunities, turn pressure into progress, and build a legacy of trust, transparency and sustainable growth.

Lead with confidence. Communicate with clarity. And remember: in the ever-evolving world of public companies, the trust you build today forms the foundation of the success you'll achieve tomorrow.

Chapter 10

Ethics in Leadership: Navigating Gray Areas in Corporate Decision-Making

In the boardroom, as in life, having ethics isn't just about knowing right from wrong -- it's about navigating the gray. As a CEO, your ability to lead with integrity when faced with ambiguous decisions not only shapes your Company's reputation and long-term viability but also plays a pivotal role in its perceived direction. Ethical leadership is more than a moral responsibility; it's a strategic imperative that you, as a CEO, are uniquely positioned to champion.

Ethical leadership has become the cornerstone of trust in a world where shareholders, employees, and the public scrutinize every move. And trust? That's the currency of business success. This chapter dives into the nuances of ethical decision-making, offering frameworks and principles to guide you when the path ahead is anything but clear.

The Stakes of Ethical Leadership

Ethical leadership isn't just about avoiding missteps but proactively building trust and resilience regardless of the circumstances and/or situation at hand.

Consider these stakes:

- **Reputational Risks:** Ethical failures can erode customer loyalty, diminish shareholder trust, and tarnish the perception of your Company that is held by any of your "publics."
- **Regulatory Consequences:** Missteps can lead to costly fines, legal challenges, personal liability… oh, and jail time.
- **Workplace Culture:** As the leader, your actions set the tone for how employees approach ethics, directly influencing morale and retention.

But here's the reality: Ethical dilemmas are rarely black and white. Often, they require choosing between complex and competing priorities, with every option having consequences.

Understanding the Ethical Gray Areas

Gray areas emerge when decisions are fraught with competing interests, ambiguous rules, or the temptation of short-term gains. Just a few examples include:

- Deciding whether layoffs are necessary to meet financial targets.
- Balancing environmental sustainability with cost pressures.
- Navigating the fine line between competitive advantage and regulatory compliance.

These are all examples of the moments when ethical leadership becomes not just important but essential.

So, let's break down a framework for ethical decision-making.

Frameworks for Ethical Decision-Making

The following are a series of suggestions to carefully consider when it's time to make a challenging decision.

Consider the Triple Bottom Line:
Evaluate decisions through the lens of:

- **Profit:** How will this impact financial performance?
- **People:** What are the consequences for employees, customers and communities?
- **Planet:** Does this decision align with short and/or long-term goals?

Example: When considering outsourcing, weigh the cost savings against potential suppliers' conditions and environmental practices.

Explore the Decision Matrix:
Ask these critical questions:

- **Is it Legal?** Ensure compliance with all laws and regulations.
- **Is it Ethical?** Does it align with your company's values and commitments? Will you personally regret the decision in the future?
- **Is it Practical?** Can this decision withstand public and stakeholder scrutiny?

Example: When pursuing tax minimization strategies, consider the reputational implications alongside legal and financial considerations. Do you have a rationale defined for the ultimate questions that will arise from Shareholders and Stakeholders – as well as the ever-inquiring media?

Stakeholder Mapping:

- Identify all stakeholders impacted by the decision.
- Assess how their interests align or conflict with the potential outcomes.

- Prioritize actions that balance benefits and harms equitably.

Example: Before implementing a price increase, evaluate its impact on customers, suppliers and shareholders. How will this be perceived? Do you have answers for the backlash?

Principles of Ethical Leadership

Ethical leadership is defined by a few key characteristics: Transparency, Accountability, Integrity and also Empathy. Let's break these down a bit.

Transparency:

- Be upfront about the rationale behind your decisions. You will be asked. Pre-consider your answers. If it's a big decision, test them with your Board of Directors and others you trust. Working with a perception analyst can help to develop potential reactions and responses that are likely to arise with all of your "publics."
- Avoid withholding critical information from Stakeholders, even when it's uncomfortable. Know that at lightning speed, they will find and publicly disclose via the Internet, social and digital media anything they think you were less than forthright about.

Accountability:

- Take responsibility for decisions and their outcomes. This is the only way you'll build trust.
- Implement oversight mechanisms, like ethics committees, to ensure integrity. While the buck stops with you as the CEO, listen carefully and consider their advice.

Integrity:

- Stand by your values, even when it's inconvenient or costly. A good night's sleep is priceless.
- Resist the temptation to compromise ethics for short-term gains.

Empathy:

- Consider the human impact of your choices. Remember the adage: "Business is personal." It's true and it is.
- Seek to understand stakeholder perspectives before finalizing decisions.

Tactics for Navigating Ethical Challenges

Navigating ethical challenges requires a tactical plan. Here are some suggestions.

Foster a Culture of Ethics:

- Model ethical behavior in your actions -- it starts at the top.
- Reward or at least publicly acknowledge employees who demonstrate integrity. This will reinforce your belief in its importance.

Engage Diverse Perspectives:

- Involve cross-functional teams and hire external advisors to uncover potential blind spots.
- Create a safe environment for employees to voice ethical concerns without fear of retaliation. It is far better for you to find out and address an issue internally than it is to read about it online or see it as the lead story of your favorite news outlet.

Leverage Technology:

- Use analytics tools to identify patterns of potential non-compliance or fraud.
- Implement AI-driven decision models to provide unbiased assessments in complex scenarios. Check these AI results using real people! Phantom data and information is real. Don't let it fool you.

Create Test Scenarios:

- Simulate decisions to evaluate their potential impacts.
- Conduct "what if" scenarios to anticipate ethical pitfalls and refine your approach.
- Have multiple "Checks and Balances" systems in place: within departments as well as in any areas you can identify as having potential vulnerabilities.

Case Study: Ethical Dilemma at NoodleNet Enterprises

NoodleNet Enterprises, a renewable energy company, faced a tough decision: Use a supplier with questionable environmental practices to meet production demands or delay delivery to find an ethical alternative.

The Process:

Stakeholder Analysis: The CEO gathered employees, investors, customers, and even some community input to weigh their priorities.

Transparency: The dilemma was disclosed to the board, with trade-offs relating to either decision clearly outlined.

Commitment to Values: Despite short-term costs, the CEO weighed all the risks that were voiced by multiple interests and decided to delay production while waiting to receive supplies from a vetted, sourced responsible supplier.

The Outcome:

NoodleNet Enterprises reinforced its brand values, gained customer loyalty and strengthened its reputation as a principled company. The short-term sacrifice paid off with long-term growth and trust. By articulating the decision and the rationale in a press release before the quarterly earnings announcement – investors, while not particularly happy, did not excessively penalize the Company. They recognized this was a short-term delay and due to a history of transparent investor relations policies, for the most part, investors continued to hold their positions as they valued the long-term prospects of NoodleNet.

Take Steps to Avoid Common Ethical Pitfalls

You'll always be challenged as a CEO in ways you cannot ever fully anticipate. However, you can take precautionary steps and have a plan to address common ethical pitfalls, including:

- **Don't Rationalize Missteps:** Avoid justifying bad decisions with excuses like "everyone else does it" or "just this once."
- **Address Small Violations:** Tackle minor ethical lapses before they snowball into more significant issues.
- **Align Incentives:** Ensure performance metrics don't encourage unethical shortcuts.

The Role of an Ethical Leader

Ethical leadership starts at the top. As a CEO, you are the moral compass of your organization.

Your responsibilities include:

- Setting clear expectations for ethical behavior.
- Providing teams with the tools and frameworks needed to navigate gray areas.
- Standing firm in your values, even when under pressure.

Key Takeaways

Ethics Is an Everyday Strategy: Integrity builds trust, and trust drives long-term success.

Be Proactive: Address ethical challenges head-on with clear frameworks and open dialogue. Offensively confronting uncomfortable issues is never easy. But being on the defense is far more uncomfortable.

Lead by Example: Your actions shape the culture and reputation of your organization.

The need to navigate gray areas is going to be inevitable in your role as a CEO, but it's also an opportunity on countless levels. By leading with heart and strategy, CEOs can transform ethical challenges into moments of trust-building and innovation. In doing so, you are laying the foundation for sustainable success, guided by principles that inspire confidence in every stakeholder…or at least a whole bunch of them! ;-)

Chapter 11

Cultivating Effective Board Relations: Alignment with Independence

With publicly traded companies, the relationship between the CEO and its Board of Directors (BOD) is more than a formality: It is a partnership that can make or break an organization's success. The board provides critical oversight, strategic counsel and a sounding board for bold ideas, while the CEO, as the leader of the company, drives execution, sets the vision and is responsible for the day-to-day operations. Yet, this dynamic is not without plenty of complexities including egos, opinions, connections, interests, liabilities and more. Balancing alignment with the board's independence requires trust, transparency and also a shared commitment to the Company's goals – defined by the CEO and ideally supported by the Board.

At its core, this complex relationship thrives when approached with both strategic precision and human connection. When CEOs lead with clarity and openness while respecting the board's fiduciary duties, the result is a partnership that inspires confidence, promotes growth and enhances governance.

The Role of the Board in Public Companies

The board's responsibilities go beyond occasional meetings -- they are the stewards of shareholder interests, ensuring the company operates responsibly and strategically. Their key roles include:

> **Strategic Oversight:** Approving transformative initiatives like mergers, acquisitions and long-term strategies.
>
> **CEO Evaluation:** Hiring, compensating, and, when necessary, replacing the CEO.
>
> **Risk Management:** Monitoring financial, legal and reputational risks while ensuring mitigation plans are in place.
>
> **Corporate Governance:** Upholding regulatory compliance and ethical standards.

For CEOs to thrive, understanding and embracing these roles by all parties is essential to building a relationship of mutual respect and trust.

Building a Strong CEO-Board Relationship

A great CEO-board relationship doesn't happen accidentally -- it's built through intentional actions, open communication and shared respect. As the proverbial saying goes: It's a two-way street.

Best practices for building a strong CEO-to-Board Relationship include all of these important aspects of perceptive communication:

Establish Trust Through Transparency:

- **Proactive Communication:** Share updates on performance, challenges and opportunities before the Board asks.

- **No Surprises:** Bring potential issues to the board early, even if they're not fully resolved. Trust thrives when the Board feels included, not blindsided. Everyone involved has liability on several fronts, and nobody wants it.
- **Accessible Data:** Ensure the Board has clear, accurate, and comprehensive information to make informed decisions.

Define Clear Roles and Boundaries:

- **Governance vs. Management:** Clearly differentiate the Board's role in oversight from the management team's responsibility for day-to-day operations.
- **Empowerment with Limits:** CEOs should involve the Board in strategic decisions without ceding control over execution.

Foster Mutual Respect:

- **Value Expertise:** Recognize and leverage each Board member's diverse skills and experiences. In fact – choose them for those very reasons.
- **Encourage Open Dialogue:** Cultivate a culture where disagreements can be voiced constructively and without fear of reprisal. Boards with a wide array of industry experiences can be priceless assets.
- **Acknowledge Contributions:** Publicly and collectively credit your Board of Directors for its role in significant achievements to reinforce the partnership.

Build Relationships Beyond the Boardroom:

- **Informal Interactions:** Retreats, dinners and casual engagements can help to foster personal connections and enhance trust with your Board members.
- **Engage Committee Chairs:** Regularly connect with key committee leaders to address concerns and maintain alignment.

Achieving Alignment While Respecting Independence

Alignment doesn't mean conformity. Alignment between the CEO and the Board of Directors is all about ensuring the Board and CEO share a unified vision while preserving -- and respecting -- the Board's autonomy. Your Board's independence is crucial as it allows for diverse perspectives, prevents groupthink and ensures robust governance. All this is ultimately in place to protect you, though it may not always feel that way.

Respecting this independence is a key aspect of the CEO-board relationship. Here are a few ways to accomplish this:

Align on Strategic Priorities:

- **Unified Vision:** Present a clear, compelling strategy that ties short-term actions to long-term goals.
- **Shared Metrics:** Use key performance indicators (KPIs) that reflect operational and strategic milestones to keep everyone focused. These can be metrics regarding financial, customer service, process, sales or marketing challenges and plans for resolution and/or progress.
- **Strategic Discussions:** Dedicate time in board meetings to identify and discuss future-focused topics rather than staying stuck on operational minutiae.

Respect Independent Oversight:

- **Encourage Constructive Criticism:** While nobody likes criticism and it's easy to resent it when coming from someone who doesn't intimately understand the day-to-day CEO stressors -- wise CEOs learn to welcome thoughtful ideas and challenges from their Board members, while possibly also asking for substantiation of their recommendations. Each challenge ultimately strengthens the CEO's decision-making thought processes and skills.
- **Leverage Diverse Perspectives:** Use the Board's independence to explore fresh insights and avoid groupthink.

- **Support Robust Governance:** Collaborate with the board to ensure vital governance processes, even if scrutiny feels uncomfortable. It is better to answer probing questions from your Board than Regulators.

Anticipate and Address Concerns:

- **Risk Management:** Keep the board informed about emerging risks and your strategies to address them. Board members have liability for decisions like you do as CEO.
- **Compensation Alignment:** Executive pay is ideally aligned with performance and shareholder interests to avoid conflicts. Often a CEO has to present their case to the Board, as the Board has the responsibility to determine CEO compensation. But by spelling out your planned milestones and proving you can/have reached them, you're positioning your compensation argument.
- **Scenario Planning:** Engage the Board in contingency planning for potential market or operational disruptions. There will be issues in any number of areas. Wise CEOs and Boards explore all possibilities -- often recruiting outside help -- knowing they will still likely be surprised by something.

Leveraging the Board's Strengths

A board isn't just there to oversee – if carefully selected and assembled, it's a strategic resource. Wise CEOs use this collective expertise and their networks to propel the company forward. Choose board members *because* of their expertise and also for their willingness to create introductions to their networks.

Use your Board as a Strategic Asset:

- Tap into board members' insights on market trends, regulatory shifts, and industry best practices.
- Leverage their networks for business development, partnerships, or talent acquisition. This is a big part of what they're paid for.

Empower Committees:

- Delegate deep dives to specialized committees, such as audit or compensation, while maintaining a clear feedback loop.
- Ensure actionable recommendations flow back to the broader board and management.

Measure Board Effectiveness:

- Just as your Board is measuring your success, regular evaluations regarding the contributions of your individual Board members should be conducted to identify strengths and areas for growth. You have to have a board and 75% of it must be independent from you and your Company. Make them work for you!
- Provide ongoing training to inform the board on governance practices and industry developments.

Case Study: Navigating Board Dynamics at Quantum Quirk Enterprises

The CEO of Quantum Quirk Enterprises faced a critical leadership test when he proposed an acquisition that split board opinion.

How the CEO Bridged the Gap:

> **Transparent Communication:** Detailed analyses and multiple Q&A sessions addressed Board concerns head-on.
>
> **Independent Validation:** A third-party consultant was brought in to assess the acquisition's assumptions and provide unbiased insights.
>
> **Joint Strategy Session:** A retreat unified the Board and CEO on broader strategic goals, ensuring the acquisition fit within the long-term vision.

Outcome:

The Board approved the acquisition, and Quantum Quirk Enterprises achieved record revenue growth twelve months from the close of the acquisition. The partnership between management and the board was cited as a key factor in the company's success because the board members with the greatest experience in integrating major acquisitions were on standby to offer the CEO advice as needed.

Key Takeaways for CEOs

> **Prioritize Communication:** Transparency and consistency are the foundation of any strong CEO - Board relationship.
>
> **Foster Alignment:** Develop shared priorities while respecting the Board's independence.
>
> **Leverage Expertise:** Treat the Board as a partner in strategy, not just a checkpoint for compliance.
>
> **Respect Independence:** Empower the Board to fulfill its fiduciary duties without compromising management authority.

The Big Picture

A high-functioning CEO - Board relationship is not just a governance requirement, but a strategic advantage. When built on trust, transparency and mutual respect, this relationship enhances decision-making, strengthens governance and positions the Company for sustainable growth. It empowers CEOs, motivates them to lead with openness and collaboration, and creates a foundation for enduring success.

Lead with openness and collaboration, and you'll gain a trusted group of partners in the Boardroom. This partnership, driven by a shared purpose and a commitment to excellence, is the key to achieving extraordinary results. It is the alignment between CEOs and Boards that elevates focused efforts while paving the way for enduring success.

Chapter 12

Succession Planning: Building a Legacy Through Seamless Leadership Transitions

As a CEO, your pivotal role in ensuring the long-term success of your company cannot be overstated. Succession planning is not just a formality -- it's a testament to your leadership, foresight and dedication to the enduring prosperity of the Company or organization. When executed effectively, succession planning not only ensures business continuity but also bolsters shareholder confidence and cultivates the next generation of leaders.

This chapter is a call to action: Approach succession planning with the same strategy and heart that define great leadership. It's about more than a plan for replacing yourself -- it's about preparing your company for a future filled with ongoing opportunities.

The Importance of Succession Planning

Succession planning isn't about anticipating an exit; it's about ensuring your company is always ready to move forward confidently. Many exits are highly unanticipated and can be downright tragically sad, having witnessed this more than once. Yet ignoring the potential of accidents, illness and deaths or other less dramatic events, won't change the fact that having a plan is essential for the Company's viability and health.

Here's why it matters:

Business Continuity:
A robust succession plan ensures stability during transitions, maintaining momentum in operations and strategy.

Shareholder Confidence:
Investors value companies that are proactive about leadership transitions. Transparent planning signals maturity (as in emotional maturity and the confidence of senior management!) and is a required risk management strategy.

Talent Development:
Succession planning is also leadership development. It nurtures a pipeline of capable executives ready to step into critical roles.

Crisis Preparedness:
Unplanned events can disrupt even the strongest companies. A well-prepared plan mitigates risks, providing a clear path forward in times of uncertainty.

Key Considerations for CEOs
Succession planning is both a strategic and a deeply human process. There are a variety of factors to consider, including but not limited to:

Align Succession Planning with Corporate Strategy:

- Define the skills and attributes needed to execute your company's vision.
- Anticipate how strategic priorities might evolve and align potential successors with future needs.

Evaluate Internal vs. External Candidates:

- **Internal Candidates:** Promote continuity and morale while leveraging institutional knowledge.
- **External Candidates:** Bring fresh perspectives and skills, particularly during transformation.

Ensure Board Engagement:

- Make succession planning a standing agenda item for board meetings.
- Leverage the board's insights to shape and evaluate your plan.

Incorporate Diversity:

- Build a leadership pipeline that reflects diverse perspectives to enhance decision-making and align with stakeholder expectations.

Define Success Criteria:

- Use clear metrics to evaluate potential successors, such as leadership style, cultural fit, and strategic thinking.

Steps to Effective Succession Planning

Succession planning is an ongoing journey, not a one-time event. Here's how to get it right:

Assess Current Leadership Needs:

- Review the CEO's responsibilities and the company's challenges.
- Identify any leadership gaps that may need to be addressed.

Build a Leadership Pipeline:

- Implement development programs that expose high-potential employees to cross-functional roles and strategic initiatives.
- Offer mentorship opportunities and stretch assignments to prepare future leaders.
- Note that this is particularly important because sometimes – during unanticipated events – interim CEOs are necessary. While the interim CEO, who is often a well-groomed employee or Board member may win the role of permanent CEO -- during the time while a search is conducted, time doesn't stop nor do investor expectations of Company performance. So, having an internal option at the ready is an important corporate health strategy.

Identify and Groom Successors:

- Use objective criteria to evaluate internal and external candidates.
- Assign challenging projects to develop skills and monitor performance over time.

Create a Transition Plan:

- Develop a detailed roadmap for the transition, including onboarding and knowledge transfer processes.
- Set clear milestones to track progress.

Communicate Transparently:

- Share the succession plan with stakeholders to build confidence.
- Manage messaging carefully to avoid speculation or uncertainty.

Test and Refine the Plan:

- Conduct simulations to identify weaknesses.
- Regularly update the plan to reflect changes in business priorities or leadership needs.

Best Practices for Seamless Leadership Transitions

There are a variety of best practices to consider implementing – continuously – during the life of any corporate entity. The ones to carefully consider are as follows:

Start Early:

Succession planning is about readiness, not urgency. Begin planning well before a transition is expected. Which means NOW because countless events cannot be planned for. Putting your head in the sand and ignoring this fact is not an option for any Company.

Engage External Advisors:

Leverage executive search firms or consultants to benchmark talent and identify potential external candidates.

Involve Outgoing CEOs:
- Facilitate a smooth handover by having the outgoing CEO mentor their successor.
- Balance involvement to avoid overshadowing the incoming leader.

Monitor Post-Transition Performance:

- Set clear metrics for the new CEO's performance.
- Offer ongoing support, such as coaching or advisory relationships with the board.

Case Study: Smooth Transition at Perpetual Pivots Inc.

Perpetual Pivots Inc., a leading software company, faced a critical leadership transition during rapid growth.

Key Success Factors included:

Early Preparation: The board and CEO had identified potential successors five years in advance.

Leadership Development: High-potential executives were provided with cross-functional assignments and executive education.

Transparent Communication: Stakeholders were informed well, ensuring trust and stability.

Seamless Handover: The outgoing CEO was an advisor for six months, supporting the new leader.

Outcome:
The transition was lauded by analysts and investors – including the Shark Smile Investor Syndicate -- and the new CEO accelerated growth with plenty of support, reinforcing shareholder confidence.

Common Executive Transitioning Pitfalls and How to Avoid Them

Having a succession plan is not optional: It is a Must-Do. That said, here are some common pitfalls that are often missed before, during and even after creating a succession plan.

- **Delaying the Planning:** It is of paramount importance to start planning early and to stay up-to-date with your plans to avoid scrambling in times of need.

- **Overreliance on a Single Candidate:** Develop a deep bench of talent to reduce vulnerability. This is an especially critical consideration because the unexpected can happen…unexpectedly!
- **Ignoring Culture Fit:** A misaligned leader can disrupt morale. So, as CEO along with your Board of Directors and others, during your selection process, you want to be sure to prioritize values and assess related alignment.
- **Lack of Board Involvement:** Engage the board to ensure accountability and alignment. And if you expect you'll get pushback or a variety of suggested candidates (and you likely will!) present this as a priority issue sooner rather than later!

Key Takeaways

> **Proactivity Is Key:** Start planning now, even if a transition isn't imminent. Life is change. Change is the only constant.
>
> **Align with Strategy:** Succession planning should reflect your company's long-term goals.
>
> **Develop Talent:** Build a leadership pipeline to ensure readiness at every level.
>
> **Communicate Effectively:** Transparency builds trust and confidence among stakeholders.

Succession planning is about more than continuity -- done correctly, it's about legacy. Preparing for seamless leadership transitions sets the stage for your company to survive and thrive under new leadership. Perceptive leaders ensure their organization's brightest days are still ahead by applying insight, strategy and heart.

Chapter 13

Transparency is Power: Building Trust and Competitive Advantage

In today's hyperconnected world, transparency isn't just about compliance but connection. It's about fostering trust, demonstrating accountability, and setting your company apart in a crowded marketplace. For leaders, transparency is more than a buzzword; it's a strategy that drives sustainable success and enhances relationships with shareholders, stakeholders and employees.

When wielded with purpose, transparency becomes your organization's competitive edge -- empowering you to show the world what your company does and why it matters.

▎*The Power of Transparency in Modern Leadership*

Understanding and prioritizing transparency is no longer optional; it is a strategic imperative for achieving credibility and resilience in competitive markets. Let's break it down.

Evolving Stakeholder Expectations:

- **Informed Investors:** Shareholders demand more than financial reports -- they expect insight into governance, ethics and social responsibility.
- **Empowered Consumers:** Today's customers favor brands that are open about supply chains, environmental impacts and societal contributions.
- **Regulatory Scrutiny:** Governments are holding companies accountable for accurate disclosures, turning transparency into a legal and strategic necessity.

Competitive Differentiation:

- **Trust as Currency:** Trust becomes the deciding factor in industries where products are similar.
- **Reputation Management:** Transparent companies weather crises better and recover faster.
- **Talent Magnetism:** Top talent gravitates to companies that align with their values and demonstrate integrity.

Benefits of Leading with Transparency

Corporate transparency is a powerful tool for building trust, enhancing reputation and driving long-term success. By openly sharing essential information with stakeholders, you build credibility, attract loyal customers and investors, and create a culture of accountability within your organization. Transparency also helps mitigate risks, strengthens relationships, and positions your company as a leader in integrity and innovation, giving you a competitive edge in today's informed and interconnected marketplace. Transparency is an asset. Let's bullet point why.

Enhanced Investor Confidence:

- Open communication builds trust and reduces uncertainty.
- Transparent companies often enjoy lower capital costs due to diminished risk.
- Honesty attracts long-term investors who prioritize sustainable growth.

Strengthened Stakeholder Relationships:

- Customers appreciate clarity about sourcing, values and impact.
- Open supplier partnerships promote innovation and collaboration.
- Transparent engagement with communities enhances corporate citizenship.

Operational Excellence:

- Transparency aligns employees with the company's mission and goals.
- Open discussions about challenges foster proactive problem-solving.
- Establishing a culture of openness encourages innovation and creativity.

Strategies to Embrace and Leverage Transparency

Here are a series of strategies you and your team can implement.

Establish Open Communication Channels:

- Go beyond required disclosures with ESG reports, updates on risk factors, and strategic initiatives.
- Use platforms like webinars, blogs and social media to connect directly with stakeholders.
- Create feedback mechanisms that show stakeholders their voices matter.

Tell Honest, Compelling Stories:

- Share your company's journey authentically, highlighting successes and lessons learned.
- Be visible as a CEO -- use interviews, blogs and public engagements to connect.
- Celebrate your impact with real-world examples that show your values in action.

Commit to Transparent Decision-Making:

- Explain the rationale behind significant choices, including risks and benefits.
- Own up to mistakes and outline steps for improvement -- accountability builds trust.
- Involve stakeholders where appropriate, fostering a culture of shared responsibility.

Strengthen Corporate Governance:

- Provide insights into your board's diversity, composition and decision-making.
- Share ethics and compliance initiatives to reinforce your company's values.
- Use independent audits to validate claims about sustainability, governance, and performance.

Overcoming Barriers to Transparency.

Transparency takes courage and it's not without challenges. Still, each obstacle presents an opportunity to reinforce your image as a bold leader. Here are some reasons why being transparent is feared -- even though it's the best choice -- and some suggested solutions for getting comfortable with more disclosure.

Fear of Negative Perception:

Solution: Shift your perspective. Being transparent about the challenges you face shows humility and builds credibility.

Competitive Concerns:

> **Solution:** While proprietary information must be protected, sharing broader strategies fosters trust without compromising your edge.

Cultural Resistance:

> **Solution:** Lead by example. When leaders model transparency, it becomes an organizational norm.

Implementing Transparency: A Blueprint for CEOs

To define a plan for greater transparency, it helps to do an internal audit to determine areas where it may be lacking. Then, define a strategy. Test it and tweak it. Get your entire team on board.

Assess Current Transparency Levels:

- Conduct an audit of disclosure practices and stakeholder perceptions.
- Identify gaps where openness could drive impact.

Develop a Transparency Strategy:

- Define clear objectives for your transparency initiatives.
- Align your efforts with your company's mission and values.

Engage Stakeholders:

- Train employees to embrace transparency with management regarding their roles.
- Invite external stakeholders to share insights on what they value.

Implement and Communicate:

- Update policies to institutionalize transparency in a non-threatening way.
- Provide regular updates through diverse channels.

Monitor and Adapt:

- Establish feedback loops to evaluate effectiveness.
- Refine efforts as the business environment evolves.

Measuring the Impact of Transparency

No policy is very good without assessing its value and worthiness. Markers for measuring the impact of greater transparency could be any or all of the following.

- **Conduct Perception Audits**: Hire a perception analyst to assess shareholder and/or stakeholder perceptions so you can stay ahead of potential issues.
- **Investor Confidence:** Track stock price stability, shareholder inquiries, and meeting participation.
- **Customer Trust:** Monitor loyalty metrics like retention rates and net promoter scores.
- **Employee Engagement:** Use surveys and turnover data to assess alignment with transparency goals.

Transparency as a Leadership Imperative

Transparency is more than a box to check -- it's a strategic advantage used by perceptive leaders. Being open about your company's successes and challenges builds trust that fuels relationships drives performance, and strengthens reputation, giving you a competitive edge as a leader.

Lead boldly, communicate openly, and make transparency a cornerstone of your leadership style. The rewards -- including trust, loyalty and lasting impact -- are well worth the effort.

Section III

Risk, Resilience and Responsibility

Chapter 14

Anticipating Risks and Leading Through Crisis:
A Leader's Playbook for Resilience

In the intricate dance of leadership, risk isn't something to fear -- it's something to understand, respect and prepare for. The stakes are high, and the spotlight is ever-present. How you anticipate and navigate risks can define your legacy and shape your organization's future.

Today enterprise risk management (ERM) isn't just a shield against crises; it's a strategic compass guiding your company toward opportunities amid uncertainty.

This chapter invites you to embrace risk management as a cornerstone of leadership. With preparation, insight and the courage to lead with clarity, you can transform challenges into milestones of success.

The Strategic Role of Risk Management in Leadership

In our interconnected world, risks manifest across multiple dimensions and, they often do so simultaneously. The most common areas of risk include:

- **Operational Risks:** From supply chain disruptions to technology failures, operational breakdowns can ripple across the organization.
- **Strategic Risks:** Market shifts, regulatory changes and new competitors can disrupt the best-laid plans.
- **Financial Risks:** Interest rate fluctuations, currency volatility and credit risks demand constant vigilance.
- **Reputational Risks:** In the age of social media, a single ethical lapse or data breach can cascade into a full-blown crisis.

When leaders take a proactive approach to risk, they do more than safeguard their organizations -- they lay the groundwork for more informed decisions, increase stakeholder trust and enhance the likelihood of long-term value. This proactive stance empowers you to be in control and steer your organization toward the success you desire.

Building a Risk-Resilient Organization

There are a variety of steps you can take to build a risk-resilient organization. Here are a series to start with.

Build a Culture of Awareness and Accountability

- **Lead by Example:** As a leader, your commitment to risk management sets the tone. Your actions, more than any policy or guideline, demonstrate their importance and influence the entire organization.
- **Integrate Risk into Strategy:** Strategic decisions should consider potential risks and mitigation plans.

- **Empower Employees:** Create an environment where employees feel safe raising concerns. Risk management thrives on open dialogue.

Master the Art of Risk Identification

- **Internal Audits:** Regularly assess vulnerabilities in operations, technology and processes.
- **External Trends:** Establish strategies to help you stay ahead by monitoring macroeconomic shifts, regulatory changes, and competitive movements.
- **Stakeholder Insights:** Employees, investors and customers often spot risks before they escalate -- engage with them actively. By actively engaging with stakeholders, CEOs can tap into their diverse perspectives and, if necessary, apply early risk detection capabilities. Doing so will enhance the organization's risk management strategy.

Categorize Risks with Precision

- **Prioritize Risks by Impact and Likelihood:** Use tools like risk matrices to focus on what matters most.
- **Key Risk Indicators (KRIs):** Establish metrics that provide real-time alerts for emerging threats.
- **Scenario Planning:** Imagine the best, worst and most likely outcomes for each critical risk.

Design Dynamic Risk Mitigation Strategies with these 4 concepts

- **Avoid:** Eliminate avoidable risks that pose high stakes.
- **Transfer:** Use insurance or strategic partnerships to share potential losses.
- **Reduce:** Strengthen controls and redundancies to lessen exposure.
- **Accept:** Embrace manageable risks that align with growth opportunities.

Leading Confidently in a Crisis

Crises are crucibles of leadership that test resilience, adaptability and integrity. To ensure readiness so you can lead more confidently in the event of a crisis, consider the following:

Stay Ahead with Preparation

- **Early Warning Systems:** Invest in predictive analytics to spot trouble before it arrives.
- **Stress Testing:** Simulate crises -- cyberattacks, natural disasters, or product recalls to hone your response strategies.
- **Crisis Playbooks:** Develop clear plans for high-priority risks, with roles and responsibilities outlined.

Respond with Clarity and Compassion

- **Assemble the A-Team:** Identify decision-makers and communicators before a crisis occurs. Be very clear about who has the authority to say what.
- **Be Transparent:** Acknowledge the issue, share your plan, and communicate frequently. This transparency builds trust and respect among stakeholders in uncertain times. They won't necessarily like the situation you're in – but they will be less hostile if they are assured that someone is taking responsibility, managing and providing updates as best as possible.
- **Stabilize, Then Strategize:** First, contain the issue. Then, focus on recovery and turning lessons into action.

Build Organizational Resilience

- **Adapt Quickly:** Be ready to pivot strategies when conditions change.
- **Strengthen Buffers:** Maintain staffing, inventory and system redundancies in case of weather disruptions.
- **Learn and Improve:** Treat every crisis as a teacher: Learn, refine processes and reinforce strengths.

Avoiding Pitfalls: Common Mistakes and How to Overcome Them

There are a variety of mistakes that commonly accompany crises that escalate. These include:

Ignoring Low-Likelihood Risks:

- **Mistake:** Underestimating rare but catastrophic events.
- **Solution:** Plan for "black swan" scenarios through stress testing.

Relying Solely on the Past:

- **Mistake:** Using historical data as the sole predictor of future risks.
- **Solution:** Combine past insights with forward-looking tools like machine learning.

Inconsistent Implementation:

- **Mistake:** Applying risk practices unevenly across departments.
- **Solution:** Standardize and regularly audit risk processes.

Fumbling Communication:

- **Mistake:** Leaving stakeholders in the dark during a crisis.
- **Solution:** Establish clear communication protocols that prioritize empathy and clarity.

Critical Takeaways for Visionary CEOs

1. **Risk is Opportunity:** When managed well, risks can unlock growth and innovation.

2. **Prepare Relentlessly:** Build resilience by anticipating and planning for the unexpected.
3. **Communicate Courageously:** Honesty and empathy are your greatest allies in both preparation and crisis.
4. **Lead with Agility:** The best leaders pivot gracefully, adapting to meet challenges head-on.
5. **Reflect and Refine:** Let each risk or crisis shape your organization's more robust, smarter future.

Effective risk management isn't about eliminating uncertainty but mastering it. By approaching risks with curiosity, confidence and preparation, you position your company to survive challenges and thrive beyond them.

Chapter 15

Cybersecurity in the Boardroom:

A Leader's Role in Data Protection and Safeguarding the Future

Cybersecurity is no longer a back-office technical issue in today's interconnected world. It is a strategic imperative that sits squarely in the boardroom. For CEOs of public companies, championing data protection is a moral and financial obligation. It's about safeguarding the organization's assets, protecting its reputation, and preserving the trust of shareholders and a very broad array of stakeholders.

Cybersecurity is not just about preventing threats -- it's about building resilience, inspiring confidence and staying ahead in a digital-first era. This chapter offers insights and checkpoints to empower you to lead your organization's cybersecurity efforts with foresight, clarity and an unwavering commitment to protection and transparency.

Why Cybersecurity Deserves a Seat in the Boardroom

The stakes have never been higher. Cyber threats are no longer a question of "ifs" but "whens." The implications of a breach can ripple far beyond the IT department: These days security leaks often land on the front pages of every major media outlet followed by courtroom appearances. They can quickly erode the public trust of partners, clients, shareholders and the public at large – all while giving your competitors a distinct public relations advantage.

Let's look at reasons why cybersecurity should be discussed, planned and assessed regularly at the Board level:

Rising Threat Landscape:

- Cyberattacks are increasingly sophisticated, targeting everything from sensitive customer data to operational infrastructure.

    The financial toll is staggering, with the average cost of a data breach exceeding $4 million across all companies and according to an article in *Trends in Cybersecurity Breach Disclosures,* the average skewed to a whopping $116 million -- All compounded by immeasurable reputational damage. This underscores the urgent need for leaders to champion data protection, as the financial implications of cyber threats can significantly impact the company's bottom line – and possibly even its viability.

Regulatory and Legal Pressures:

- Laws are already in place regarding data collection and how it is used. For example, the General Data Protection Regulation (GDPR) of the European Union, aims to protect the privacy of individuals' personal data. Then there's the California Consumer Privacy Act (CCPA), a US state law specifically designed to protect the privacy of California residents' personal data. Both regulations give individuals more control over how companies collect, use, and share their information. Expect more regulations to come.

Key points to consider under each include:

> **Scope:** GDPR applies to all companies processing data of EU residents, while CCPA only applies to companies operating in California.
>
> **Key rights:** Both regulations grant individuals the right to access their data, request deletion, and object to certain data processing activities.
>
> **Consent:** GDPR generally requires explicit consent for data processing, while CCPA takes a more flexible approach depending on the type of data.
>
> **Enforcement:** Companies that violate GDPR can face significant fines, while CCPA also includes penalties for non-compliance.

NOTE: Under both, Boards and executives may face personal liability if found negligent in cybersecurity oversight.

> **Shareholder Demands:** Investors recognize cybersecurity's direct impact on valuation and risk. Transparent strategies are now a baseline expectation.
>
> **Operational Continuity and Competitive Edge:** A single attack can disrupt critical operations, jeopardizing customer trust and revenue. Conversely, a robust cybersecurity posture differentiates companies as trustworthy and forward-thinking leaders in their fields.

▪ *The Leader's Role in Cybersecurity Leadership*

If you're at the helm, you are the steward of the company's cybersecurity strategy. Your influence can elevate data protection from a technical necessity to a cultural and strategic advantage. Your role is not just to work with others to approve budgets and strategies but to actively champion a culture of security and ensure that cybersecurity is a recurring agenda item in board meetings.

So, what can you do?

Champion a Culture of Security:

- Show that cybersecurity is not just an IT issue but a company-wide priority. Your advocacy sets the tone for the entire organization.
- Reinforce the message that everyone -- from the boardroom to the breakroom -- is involved in protecting data and systems.

Elevate Cybersecurity in Board Discussions:

- "Risk" brings cybersecurity to the forefront by ensuring it's a recurring agenda item in board meetings.
- Push for dedicated expertise, whether through cyber-savvy board members, ongoing education, or whatever else is a necessary budget item.

Align Cybersecurity with Business Goals:

- Integrate data protection into broader strategies like digital transformation, mergers, or new product launches. Recruit the expertise you need.
- Translate technical risks into clear, actionable insights that the board and stakeholders can understand.

Demonstrate Personal Accountability:

- Advocate for the necessary budget and resources to protect against evolving threats.
- Embrace best practices yourself, setting a personal example of compliance and commitment.

Crafting a Comprehensive Cybersecurity Strategy

Building resilience begins with a thoughtful, systematic approach to managing risks. Let's review an outline of steps to carefully consider.

1. **Identify and Assess Risks:**

    - Pinpoint the assets -- the data, systems and processes that are most critical to your business.
    - Map out the threat landscape for your specific industry, as well as your company and operations.

2. **Build a Strong Governance Framework:**

    - Develop clear policies and procedures for data handling and incident response. Don't just expect them to be followed: Inspect that they are followed.
    - Delineate roles between the board, executives, and IT leaders to ensure accountability.
    - Have checks and balances systems in place – for example, make sure that key passwords are accessible and maybe even double verifiable, in the event your IT person unceremoniously decides to exit.

3. **Prepare for the Inevitable:**

    - Design and regularly update an incident response plan.
    - Establish backups and redundancies.
    - Conduct simulations and stress tests to rehearse how the organization will respond under pressure.
    - Inspect and Test.

4. **Commit to Continuous Improvement:**

    o   Use real-time monitoring and analytics to stay ahead of potential threats.
    o   Regularly audit firewalls and systems to identify and close vulnerabilities.
    o   Train employees at all levels, ensuring they understand how to recognize and mitigate risks.

Communicating Cybersecurity with Transparency

Building trust internally and externally requires more than action -- it demands excellence in communication. You'll want to assure all of your "publics" that they can trust their personal and/or private data with you and that your company has systems in place to keep confidential information confidential. To build this trust, carefully consider the following:

Investors and Shareholders:

- Keep investors informed about cybersecurity initiatives, using metrics to demonstrate preparedness and impact.
- Acknowledge vulnerabilities and outline steps to address them, showing proactive management.

Customers:

- Be honest about your commitment to safeguarding data. Transparency strengthens trust, even in challenging times.
- Should a breach occur, communicate promptly and clearly about the resolution process.

Employees:

- Equip your teams with the knowledge they need to protect data daily. Recognize and reward their contributions to cybersecurity.

Inspiring Confidence Through Cybersecurity

The ability to manage cyber risks is no longer a competitive advantage -- it's a leadership necessity. CEOs who prioritize cybersecurity send a powerful message: That their organizations are ready to navigate the complexities of the digital age with strength, strategy and forthright integrity.

Key Takeaways for CEOs:

> **Treat Cybersecurity as Strategy:** This isn't just about protection -- it's about positioning your company as a leader in trust and innovation.
>
> **Own the Narrative:** Your leadership and transparency set the tone for stakeholders' perception of your data protection commitment.
>
> **Invest in Resilience:** From cutting-edge technology to employee training, the best defenses require thoughtful, sustained investment.
>
> **Communicate Courageously:** Whether in proactive discussions or crisis management, openness builds bridges of trust that weather any storm.
>
> **Lead with Vision:** Cybersecurity is about safeguarding the present while empowering the future. Your actions today shape your organization's legacy for tomorrow.

By championing cybersecurity -- at every level of your organization -- you will be protecting key assets; inspiring the confidence of shareholders and stakeholders; better enabling innovation; and, laying the foundation for enduring success.

Chapter 16

Leadership in Crisis:

Principles for Navigating the Unexpected with Composure and Care

Crises, the ultimate test of leadership, require leaders to navigate turbulent times with a sense of composure. This composure paired with thoughtful actions, not only defines the organization's resilience but may also shape its legacy. Whether it's a financial shock, reputational fallout, operational disruption, or global upheaval, the ability to maintain composure, make decisive decisions, and inspire trust is key to effective crisis leadership.

This chapter provides actionable principles for leading with grace and grit when the unexpected strikes. Crisis management is about way more than just damage control -- it's about seizing the opportunity to lead with vision, rally your organization, and emerge stronger than before.

The Leader's Role in a Crisis: A Crucial Responsibility

Your crisis leadership presence must be strategic and deeply human. Your responsibilities are clear:

> **Set the Tone:** Your calm and confident demeanor is the bedrock of stability for your team.
>
> **Unify the Team:** Foster alignment and purpose among your leadership team and all employees.
>
> **Communicate Transparently:** Build trust by maintaining honest, timely communication with shareholders and stakeholders.
>
> **Drive Action:** Balance quick decisions with long-term foresight, ensuring the organization moves forward with intention.

Principles of Inspiring Crisis Leadership

During any crisis, you will quite likely not have all the information you need when you need it. It's helpful to remember this great quote by General Colin Powell: "The news is never as good or as bad as the first report."

Your job is to act like a leader by assuring others that you are taking charge while directing your team to gather all the information possible, so you can make the most informed leadership decisions – which will quite possibly be made as the players and situations evolve in real-time. To do this effectively, consider these principles embraced by leaders in a crisis.

Embrace the Role of Crisis Leader

- **Own the Situation:** Taking responsibility both publicly and internally establishes trust.

- **Be a Steady Presence:** Show up visibly and consistently, signaling your commitment to guiding the organization through the storm.
- **Lead with Empathy:** Crises usually impact people, whether employees, customers and/or communities. Acknowledge their struggles and meet them with compassion as best as possible.

Stay Composed Under Pressure

- **Resilience Starts with You:** Manage your stress to avoid reactive or impulsive decision-making.
- **Anchor in Facts:** Stick to reliable data and trusted sources, avoiding the noise of speculation. Crises require leaders to utilize their most objective skills while harnessing emotions as best as possible.
- **Be Agile:** Adapt to new developments while keeping an eye on long-term objectives.

Communicate Clearly and Transparently

- **Keep Teams Informed:** Regular, honest updates to employees build trust and align efforts.
- **Address Stakeholders:** Proactive communication with shareholders, customers and the public can reassure each respective audience of the Company's plans, direction and viability.
- **Balance Honesty and Hope:** Acknowledge the gravity of the crisis while providing a vision for recovery and resilience.

Leverage Expertise

- **Build a Crisis Team:** Engage leaders with the right skills and bring in external advisors when needed. Objective insight from "an outsider" can make a huge difference in bringing a broader perspective to the situation.

- **Encourage Collaboration:** Diverse input prevents blind spots and stimulates innovative solutions.
- **Trust the Data:** Let analytics and informed insights guide your choices when possible.

Act Decisively

- **Prioritize Urgently:** Identify critical tasks and allocate resources to address them immediately.
- **Delegate with Trust:** Empower your team to execute while maintaining oversight.
- **Be Transparent About Tough Choices:** Clearly explain the reasoning behind decisions, especially those involving sacrifices.

Build for Long-Term Resilience

- **Debrief Post-Crisis:** Review what worked, what didn't, and how the organization can improve its preparedness.
- **Rebuild Confidence:** Demonstrate accountability and take visible steps to address root causes.
- **Innovate and Adapt:** Look for opportunities to strengthen operations and reposition for future growth.

Navigating Specific Types of Crises

Crises come in all kinds of disguises and they are never pleasant. They often force a leader's hand – requiring hard decisions that are sure to be unpopular. Here are a few types of potential crises to consider. Perhaps by reading them here, you can recognize their potential impact – ideally before they make an appearance. At the least, start to familiarize yourself with their traits to become somewhat better prepared.

Financial Crises

- Assess liquidity immediately and implement cost-control measures to stabilize finances.
- Maintain transparent communication with investors and creditors, reinforcing confidence in leadership.
- Revisit strategy to identify areas for divestment or focused investment.

Operational Disruptions

- Activate contingency plans to minimize downtime and service disruptions.
- Collaborate with suppliers and partners to address vulnerabilities in the supply chain.
- Prioritize employee well-being and ensure their safety throughout the disruption.

Reputational Crises

- Take control of the narrative by responding quickly and factually to misinformation.
- Own any mistakes, apologize where necessary, and outline concrete corrective actions.
- Invest in brand rebuilding through actions that demonstrate renewed integrity and trustworthiness.
- Remember – the blame game doesn't work. As a leader, you're in charge. Your public will expect you to respond accordingly. So, take charge: Say you are "working on solving the problem; finding a resolution; and/or preventing it from happening again." Blaming anyone for the issue will backfire – then you'll have a bigger crisis to deal with.

Industry-Wide or Global Crises

- Evaluate multiple potential outcomes and craft contingency plans for each scenario.
- Collaborate with industry peers and public entities to address common challenges.
- Pivot strategies and adapt operations to align with new realities in the market.

Case Study: Zap Zing Widgets Inc. -- Rising from Crisis

When a product recall threatened to erode Zap Zing Widgets' reputation, its leadership team turned a potential disaster into an example of resilience.

Key Actions:

1. **Immediate Response:** The CEO publicly acknowledged the issue, committed to customer safety, and mobilized a dedicated recall team.
2. **Transparent Communication:** Regular updates were shared with stakeholders, and the CEO appeared in media interviews to take responsibility.
3. **Long-Term Commitment:** Zap Zing overhauled its quality controls and invested in regular independent audits, which helped to rebuild trust through visible actions.

Outcome:

While the recall temporarily impacted Zap Zing's stock price, the decisive and transparent leadership measures ultimately restored confidence. Within a year, the company regained its market position and saw an increase in customer loyalty.

Actionable Steps for Leaders and their Teams

Develop a Crisis Management Plan: Identify protocols, roles and resources for handling crises effectively.

Practice with Simulations: Test readiness with mock scenarios to uncover gaps and refine strategies.

Build a Cross-Functional Crisis Team: Include representatives from key areas like finance, operations, legal and communications.

Communicate Frequently: Use every available channel to update stakeholders honestly and clearly.

Support Stakeholders: Prioritize the well-being of employees and customers, offering tangible resources where needed.

Key Takeaways for CEOs

Your Composure is a Beacon: Remaining calm and focused inspires confidence throughout the organization.

Communication is Your Superpower: Clear, transparent messaging is essential to maintaining trust.

Collaboration Unlocks Solutions: Engage experts and stakeholders to effectively uncover opportunities and navigate challenges.

Crisis = Growth Opportunity: Every challenge provides lessons to strengthen resilience and improve future readiness.

Crises are inevitable, but they can be transformative with the right mindset and strategies. By leading with clarity, empathy and vision, you can guide your organization through uncertainty, protect its value, and lay the foundation for an even brighter future.

Chapter 17

Navigating Climate and Sustainability Risks:

Addressing Regulations, Politics, and Activist Shareholders

In a world increasingly shaped by activists and regulators touting environmental and sustainability concerns, the role of being a leader in charge extends beyond driving profit -- it's about safeguarding and securing a future-ready organization. From navigating complex regulations to addressing activist shareholder demands, leading with sustainability at the forefront is both a challenge and an opportunity. (And yes, sometimes a pain in the arse, but if you want to be the leader, you'll just have to deal with it!)

This chapter explores how CEOs can embrace environmental stewardship, leverage it as a competitive edge, and address evolving expectations with transparency, foresight, and innovation.

Why Sustainability is Non-Negotiable for Leaders

Sustainability policies are nonnegotiable for leaders today due to a variety of factors that ebb and flow, causing both up and down challenges, often based on political landscapes as well as the rise of activist investors, that are ever-dynamic. Here are a few you'll need to prepare for:

Regulatory Pressures

- **Evolving Standards:** Governments worldwide are introducing stricter emissions caps and mandatory reporting frameworks, such as the EU Corporate Sustainability Reporting Directive (CSRD) laws that require large companies and public-interest entities to report on their environmental and social impact and also the Security and Exchange Commission's (SEC) climate disclosure proposals.
- **Financial Impact:** Regulations like carbon taxes and sustainability incentives are reshaping how companies allocate resources and are forced to measure performance.
- **Corporate Accountability:** C-suite leaders are increasingly held accountable for ensuring their organizations meet stringent environmental compliance.

Political Dynamics

- **Policy Fluctuations:** Changing political administrations can alter sustainability priorities, creating an unpredictable regulatory landscape…and oh so much fun…not.
- **Geopolitical Considerations:** Climate policies intersect with trade, national security and resource management, demanding careful navigation.

Activist Shareholders & Stakeholders

- **Amplified Demands:** Activist funds as well as an assortment of public constituents are prioritizing climate action, pushing for transparent reporting,

emissions reductions and green innovations. Face it: Many of these are short-sighted, knee-jerk reactions. However, this won't change the fact that you may have to comply or face the consequences of non-compliance.
- **Proxy Challenges:** Shareholders not aligned with stated (or not stated) corporate environmental, social, and governance (ESG) efforts are increasingly leveraging their power to influence strategic shifts aligned with their preferred agendas.

Evolving Market Expectations

- **Consumer Trends:** Customers are prioritizing eco-conscious brands, transforming sustainability from a preference into a baseline expectation. They can also be quite vocal (reasonably -- or not) on social media.
- **Employee Advocacy:** The next generation of employees appears to be actively seeking workplaces that align with their values, particularly environmental responsibility.

The Cost of Inaction

Failing to address sustainability risks can have severe consequences. They are not limited to the following:

- **Financial Penalties:** From fines by regulators to assets stranded in foreign lands, neglecting climate considerations can decrease profitability.
- **Eroded Trust:** Negative press, social media campaigns led by activists and/or consumer boycotts that begin due to interpretations of corporate practices perceived to be "anti-sustainability" can quickly put a Company in defensive mode and simultaneously damage its image and brand(s).
- **Strategic Vulnerability:** Resistance to adopting sustainable practices could mean falling behind competitors already positioned as green leaders.

The Leader's Role in Leading Sustainability

So, what is a leader to do? Here are a variety of ideas to carefully consider.

Embed Sustainability into Corporate Strategy

- **Vision with Action:** Integrate sustainability goals into your Company's broader purpose and long-term business model.
- **Tailored Approaches:** Conduct materiality assessments to identify your industry's most impactful environmental issues.
- **Holistic Adoption:** Encourage collaboration across departments -- from supply chain and product design to marketing and everything and everyone in between -- to ingrain sustainability into every business function.

Engage and Empower the Board

- **Expertise in ESG:** Ensure board representation includes members with deep environmental, social and governance knowledge.
- **Accountability:** Regularly update the board with clear data on environmentally-related risks, opportunities and progress.
- **Collaborative Oversight:** Encourage active board participation in crafting and overseeing sustainability initiatives.

Set a Personal Example

- **Visible Commitment:** Announce bold, science-backed goals for pro-environmental policies including emissions reductions and net-zero timelines.
- **Concrete Actions:** Demonstrate leadership by initiating tangible changes, such as adopting renewable energy sources or eliminating single-use plastics and/or packaging within operations.
- **Industry Alliances:** Partner with global organizations, NGOs, and competitors to drive industry-wide progress.

Tackling Regulatory and Activist Pressures

Regulators and Activist interactions are rarely celebrated. That said, they can be more pleasant if you have a plan. So let's break the pressures down categorically.

Navigating Regulations

To best navigate regulations, leaders will want to identify ways they can be proactive, leverage the possible tax or other benefits and analyze potential scenarios to determine the best go-forward plans.

- **Be Proactive:** Navigating regulations will require an ongoing plan to monitor global climate policy changes so that leadership teams can anticipate impacts and opportunities – or at least be on top of those in the regions within which your corporation operates.
- **Leverage Benefits:** Whenever possible, you'll want to have someone monitoring these changes so that you can take advantage of green subsidies, tax credits, and partnerships for innovation.
- **Scenario Analysis:** Prepare for regulatory shifts by modeling multiple outcomes to future-proof business strategies.

Addressing Activist Shareholders

I've never met a leader who gets excited about engaging with activist shareholders. However, I've also never met a successful leader who ignores activists, either. To best manage activists, the following ideas are a good starting place.

- **Open Conversations:** Engage with activists early to discuss concerns and align on actionable goals.
- **Conduct a Perception Analysis:** Hire a competent perception analyst to assess and interpret the full array of potential perspectives that may impact your company and its initiatives. This information is powerful as it will enable you to refine messaging and get ahead of possible threats to your company.

- **Remember that Transparency is Key:** Regularly disclose your ESG milestones and also roadblocks. This will help to instill confidence that you're listening and taking action.
- **Defense Mechanisms:** Build coalitions with long-term investors who believe in the organization's sustainability commitments. Work on this *before* you need their support.

Actionable Strategies for Leaders

Let's review strategies you can begin implementing now since it's quite likely environmentally- and sustainability-based regulations are not going away – though they will likely keep shifting based on activist and political pressures.

> **Conduct an Environmental Risk Assessment:** Assess how environmental issues may impact your Company's financial performance, operations and brand perception.
>
> **Build a Comprehensive ESG Strategy: To enhance** credibility whenever possible, try to familiarize and align your corporate efforts with global frameworks like the Task Force on Climate-related Financial Disclosures (TCFD), a framework focused specifically on reporting climate-related financial risks and opportunities, and the Global Reporting Initiative (GRI), which provides a broader framework for reporting on a wide range of sustainability issues, including environmental, social, and governance aspects.
>
> **Amplify Stakeholder Communication:** Publish annual sustainability reports and host shareholder ESG reviews to highlight progress.
>
> **Foster Partnerships for Collective Progress:** Work alongside peers, government bodies, and maybe even related non-profit organizations to find ways to innovate together.

Key Takeaways for CEOs

Sustainability is Non-Negotiable: Treat pro-environmental actions as integral aspects of business success, not merely a checkpoint on your public relations initiatives.

Be the Catalyst for Change: Lead with bold commitments and inspire your team with actionable efforts. Something very simple like reminding your employees to turn off the lights makes a simple statement – while making people own the idea of taking responsibility.

Embrace Transparency: Authenticity builds trust -- own your progress and challenges.

Focus on Opportunity: Use sustainability as a competitive advantage to attract investors, customers and employees.

Sustainability isn't a trend and it is not going away. Leaders who embrace sustainability policies mitigate risks and create lasting value for their organizations and the world. Leadership in this arena isn't just good business; it's a legacy.

Section IV
Innovation and Adaptation

Chapter 18

Leading Digital Transformation:

Adapting, Igniting & Driving Technological Innovation for Resilience and Growth

In today's technology-driven landscape, digital transformation is not just a strategy -- it is a strategic lifeline for organizations seeking to remain competitive, efficient and future-ready. For C-suite leaders of public companies, steering the digital evolution means cultivating a vision that aligns technology with business objectives, fostering a culture of innovation, and ensuring organization-wide adaptability.

This chapter is your guide to championing transformative initiatives at scale, creating lasting impact through bold leadership, and positioning your company as a front-runner in the digital economy.

Why Digital Transformation Demands Leadership from the Top

Digital transformation consists of all of the strategic and systematic processes where the organization leverages digital technologies, data and innovation to fundamentally change its operations, business models, and customer interactions. This transformation aims to enhance efficiency, drive growth, deliver superior shareholder value, and ensure competitiveness in an increasingly digital economy.

Key Aspects of Digital Transformations include:

> **Integration of Technology**: Incorporating advanced technologies like cloud computing, artificial intelligence, automation, IoT and data analytics into core business processes and functions.
>
> **Creating Operational Efficiencies**: Streamlining operations to reduce costs, improve productivity, and enhance decision-making capabilities through real-time data insights.
>
> **Defining Customer-Centric Approaches**: Using digital platforms to better understand and engage with customers, provide personalized experiences, and meet evolving customer expectations.
>
> **Identifying New Revenue Streams**: Developing innovative products, services or business models that are enabled by digital capabilities, such as subscription services or e-commerce expansions.
>
> **Adapting Cultural Changes**: Encouraging an agile, innovation-driven mindset within the organization to adapt to digital trends and respond quickly to market changes.
>
> **Improving Governance and Compliance**: Ensuring digital initiatives align with regulatory requirements, cybersecurity standards, and transparency expectations for stakeholders and shareholders.

Why Digital Transformation Matters for Public Companies:

Digital transformation for any company is not merely a technological upgrade but a holistic shift that holds the potential to reshape the company's operational, strategic and even cultural dimensions. In the process of adopting digital transformations, a company becomes better positioned to not just survive but to thrive in a digital-first world. While these changes can be quite costly, while also being accompanied by plenty of resistance from every employee for any number of reasons -- falling behind and not staying on top of the ever-changing digital landscape can be even more expensive and risky. So, to get you more enrolled, let's look at the plusses and why you'll want to have a plan to stay on top of myriad digital transformations.

Unlocking Competitive Advantages

- **Data-Powered Insights:** Analytics and AI can enable businesses to respond to challenges quickly and precisely, turning information into actionable strategies.
- **Customer-Centric Solutions:** Digital platforms can enhance personalization, build loyalty, and create frictionless customer experiences.
- **Operational Excellence:** Automation can eliminate inefficiencies, lower costs, and bolster productivity across operations.

Staying Ahead of Industry Disruption

- **Rapid Innovation:** The pace of technological change is accelerating. Every day business models are challenged which elevates the importance of agility.
- **Global Reach:** Digital tools enable businesses to expand rapidly and compete globally, regardless of size or geography.

Meeting Elevated Stakeholder Expectations

- **Investor Demands:** Shareholders seek growth that hinges on technological enablement and forward-thinking strategies.

- **Workforce Evolution:** A tech-savvy workforce expects intuitive systems that empower collaboration and creativity as well as their ability to perform in their roles.

Principles for Leading Digital Transformation

There are a variety of principles worth considering when considering the undertaking of a digital transformation of any kind. Here are some noteworthy ideas to contemplate.

Create a Unified Vision

- **Define a Strategic Focus:** Link digital transformation to overarching corporate goals such as growth, market leadership and/or operational efficiency.
- **Share the "Why":** Explain the purpose and benefits of the transformation to gain buy-in from employees, investors and customers alike.
- **Outcome Orientation:** Prioritize projects with measurable returns, whether through cost reductions, revenue gains, or market share growth.

Build Resilient Governance

- **Identify Dedicated Leadership:** Appoint a Chief Digital Officer or establish a task force responsible for driving and tracking digital initiatives.
- **Outline Cross-Functional Alignment:** Involve key stakeholders from IT, marketing, finance and operations to create synergies and break silos.
- **Create Accountability Structures:** Define clear roles and key metric indicators (KPIs), and outline and refine decision-making processes to ensure cohesive execution.

Foster an Innovation-First Culture

- **Embrace Experimentation as a Norm:** Empower teams to test ideas without fear of failure, emphasizing learning over perfection within boundaries.

- **Upskill for the Future:** Invest in training to ensure all employees -- from entry-level to executive -- are equipped for the digital era.
- **Celebrate Change Agents:** Recognize and reward individuals and teams that drive innovation and adapt to new systems.

Invest in Scalable Technologies

- **Cloud Platforms:** Adopting robust cloud-based infrastructures enables flexibility, scalability and potentially cost savings.
- **Artificial Intelligence:** Harness AI to personalize customer journeys, optimize processes, and predict trends.
- **Integrated Data Systems:** Consolidate and secure data for actionable insights and streamlined decision-making.

Champion Change Management

- **Set a Structured Approach:** Develop a roadmap addressing technical deployment and organizational adaptation.
- **Share Transparent Updates:** Keep all stakeholders informed about timelines, successes and roadblocks.
- **Acknowledge Incremental Progress:** Launch initiatives in phases, testing and iterating to maximize impact and minimize risk.

Steps for Executing Large-Scale Digital Initiatives

Initiating any large-scale digital initiative is a commitment that requires a plan. Here are a variety of items worthy of careful consideration.

Evaluate Current Readiness

- Conduct a technology audit to identify redundancies and upgrade opportunities.
- Assess workforce capabilities and establish training programs to close skill gaps.

- Benchmark your current digital maturity against competitors and industry standards.

Craft a Roadmap

- Prioritize initiatives based on alignment with strategic goals and expected returns on your investments.
- Establish clear milestones to maintain momentum and track progress.
- Earmark or secure funding that reflects the scope and importance of the planned transformation.

Secure Buy-In Across Stakeholders

- **Board Engagement:** Align senior leadership with the vision and allocate resources effectively – this includes both the people power and financing necessary for upgrades.
- **Employee Inclusion:** Empower teams by involving them in planning and implementation.
- **Customer Insights:** Leverage customer feedback to ensure solutions meet their evolving needs.

Partner for Success

- Request proposals from a variety of leading technology providers to access cutting-edge solutions. Compare and contrast all submissions. Check references.
- Consider forging alliances with startups and innovators to accelerate development.
- Use external consultants to guide seamless integration and adoption.

Monitor and Evolve

- Utilize real-time analytics to assess performance, identify bottlenecks and adjust as needed.
- Continuously gather feedback to refine tools and strategies.
- Plan for scalability to ensure that the systems you select can evolve alongside business growth and industry shifts.

Overcoming Challenges in Digital Transformation

Change is not easy and when it comes to getting support and buy-in for any digital transformation, expect resistance. While most want access to the newest and the best technology features, there will always be a new learning curve that has to be scaled.

Let's address the challenges leaders are up against.

Resistance to Change

- **The Problem:** Fear and uncertainty may slow adoption.
- **The Solution:** Build confidence through transparent communication and hands-on training.

Limited Resources

- **The Problem:** Budget constraints can delay progress.
- **The Solution:** Launch pilot projects demonstrating clear ROI to justify further investment.

Siloed Data and Systems

- **The Problem:** Fragmented infrastructure hinders integration.
- **The Solution:** Establish unified platforms that streamline and centralize data management.

Cybersecurity Risks

- **The Problem:** Digital expansion increases vulnerability.
- **The Solution:** Deploy advanced cybersecurity measures, including encryption, firewalls, and frequent audits.

Key Takeaways for Leaders

Champion the Change: Your commitment sets the tone for organizational adoption and enthusiasm.

Integrate Strategy and Technology: Digital initiatives should always serve overarching business goals. Define your rationale for the long-term while choosing systems and partners capable of adapting to inevitable future needs, developments and capability advances.

Empower People: Equip employees with skills and tools to embrace any transformations confidently. Be sure that any digital upgrades include a budget for training and upskilling.

Stay Agile: Continuously refine processes and systems to adapt to emerging trends. While the "latest and greatest" may not be the best choice – delaying digital technology upgrades may ultimately prove to be over-costly as it can cause all kinds of networking glitches on many levels.

Digital transformation is not just about keeping up -- it's about forging ahead. Leaders can turn technology into a competitive advantage by approaching their roles with clarity, purpose and resilience, ensuring their organizations thrive in an ever-evolving world.

Chapter 19

Harnessing AI for Smarter Decisions:

A Leader's Guide in the Age of Artificial Intelligence

In today's fast-paced business world, Artificial Intelligence (AI) is no longer a futuristic concept but a transformative force reshaping decision-making and strategy. For leaders, AI is not just a tool but a strategic advantage and a competitive necessity that if harnessed can propel them ahead of the competition curve. The power of AI lies in its ability to analyze data, streamline operations, predict outcomes, and uncover opportunities with unmatched precision and speed: The combination of abilities gives forward-thinking leaders an edge in their decision-making. Certainly, as AI continues to be developed, its myriad potential for use in business will advance, as well – far beyond what can be imagined and applied at the time of this writing.

But, regardless, as with all powerful technologies, AI comes with challenges that can be predicted today and will likely compound in the future. Ethical dilemmas, skills, data biases, and over-reliance risk require leaders to approach AI adoption with wisdom and balance. Then, there is also phantom information that must be sorted through to avoid potentially dangerous errors and costly miscalculations.

This chapter equips leaders with actionable strategies to integrate AI responsibly and effectively into decision-making processes to potentially drive value while upholding trust and integrity. It's important to note that AI adoption also carries potential risks such as job displacement, upskilling voids, misuse of personal data and more – all of which should be carefully considered and managed.

Why AI is Essential for Decision-Making

AI offers smart leaders a variety of benefits that can enhance decision-making across multiple departments. Here are a few of those benefits.

Potential to Unlock New Insights with Enhanced Data Analysis

- **Real-Time Intelligence:** AI instantaneously processes massive amounts of data, empowering leaders to respond to market dynamics in real time. It works well now and is getting better by the second.
- **Trend Spotting:** Machine learning uncovers patterns and correlations, possibly less visible to the human eye which can fuel better forecasting and planning.
- **Proactive Decision-Making:** AI-based predictive analytics equip leaders with foresight, enabling them to anticipate risks and opportunities before they materialize.

Simplifying Routine Operations Through Automation

- **Effortless Efficiency:** From fraud detection to supply chain management, AI can be designed to automate repetitive tasks, freeing up resources for other strategic initiatives.

- **Error Reduction:** Automated processes can deliver consistency and precision, potentially minimizing costly human errors.

Deepening Customer Engagement

- **Hyper-Personalization:** AI-driven algorithms can be directed to curate individualized product recommendations and marketing strategies, enhancing customer satisfaction.
- **Voice of the Customer:** Sentiment analysis tools can decipher customer feedback, helping companies proactively refine offerings and address concerns.

Empowering Strategic Planning

- **Scenario Simulations:** Leaders can run "what-if" models to test the impact of various strategies, to gain greater confidence in their decisions.
- **Risk Optimization:** AI can add another dimension to evaluations of complex variables while presenting data-backed options for navigating uncertainty and mitigating risks.

Real-World Applications of AI Across Industries

Let's look at actual applications that are already being deployed by a variety of companies.

AI is Revolutionizing Operations and Supply Chain

- **Demand Precision:** AI is accurately forecasting demand, ensuring optimal inventory levels and eliminating waste.
- **Seamless Logistics:** Advanced routing algorithms are being used to streamline shipping, reducing costs and enhancing delivery reliability.

Transforming Financial Management

- **Smart Risk Assessment:** Creditworthiness evaluations powered by AI are being broadly used to reduce defaults and improve lending precision.
- **Fraud Protection:** Machine learning is flagging unusual transactions and as a result safeguarding assets and customer trust in real time.

Elevating Human Resources

- **Efficient Recruitment:** AI is being used to sift through resumes, identifying top candidates quickly and fairly.
- **Retention Intelligence:** Predictive tools highlight employee dissatisfaction patterns, enabling proactive engagement.

Personalizing Marketing and Sales

- **Customer Insights:** AI has been used for several years to segment audiences into precise profiles, powering targeted campaigns with higher conversion rates.
- **Future Forecasts:** AI sales prediction tools can align production and marketing efforts with upcoming trends.

Accelerating R&D Innovation

- **Faster Prototyping:** AI is accelerating the design and testing of products, and consequently, shortening time-to-market cycles.
- **Scientific Discovery:** In fields like pharmaceuticals, AI reveals potential breakthroughs that traditional methods may overlook.

Challenges of AI and How to Overcome Them

AI is not without challenges. Let's break down some of those challenges and identify the respective risks and rewards.

Data Quality and Bias
- **The Risk:** AI is only as good as the data it learns from; incomplete or biased data can distort results. Further, AI data can create false data. At the most elementary levels, mid-2024 comparisons of responses to identical questions asked between ChatGPT 4.0 vs. X's Grok have proven the impact of bias on answers, time and again.
- **The Solution:** Regularly audit and clean data, ensuring diversity and accuracy to reduce bias. Always add a careful human assessment of the data to identify false or phantom information.

Overdependence on Algorithms
- **The Risk:** Blind faith in AI can lead to poor decisions, especially in nuanced or high-stakes situations.
- **The Solution:** Use AI to complement human expertise, fostering collaboration between technology and intuition. Every situation should consider objective and subjective analysis while weighing the validity of both.

Complexity and Transparency Issues
- **The Risk:** "Black-box" algorithms can obscure decisions, eroding trust. A black box is a form of artificial intelligence that is not transparent to end users. While the user can input data and receive output, they cannot see the system's code or "logic."
- **The Solution:** Prioritize explainable AI, choosing models that offer clarity in their outputs and decisions.

Ethical and Compliance Pitfalls
- **The Risk:** Unchecked AI applications can unintentionally perpetuate discrimination in any number of ways. Consequently, it adds the potential for misuse of personal data.

- **The Solution:** Implement strict governance frameworks and adhere to global data protection standards.

Resistance to Adoption

- **The Risk:** Employees may resist AI adoption for fear of job displacement or unfamiliarity.
- **The Solution:** Focus on upskilling and engaging teams to see AI as a collaborator, not a replacement. Encourage teams to view AI as "extra brainpower" and administrative assistance.

Best Practices for Implementing AI

If you're ready to begin implementing AI to accelerate your Company's productivity and growth, consider each of these best practices.

Define Clear Goals

- Start with specific, measurable problems aligning intended results with the company's overall mission.
- Avoid "tech for tech's sake" by focusing on practical outcomes like revenue growth or improved efficiency.

Build a Solid Data Foundation

- Invest in data governance to ensure reliability and security.
- Actively identify and address biases in datasets to maintain ethical integrity.

Strike a Balance Between Automation and Oversight

- Use AI to augment human judgment rather than replace it, especially in critical decision-making areas. AI is frothing with phantom and false information.

If you ever choose to avoid human editing and careful review, you will be proceeding at your own peril.
- Train leadership teams to interpret AI-driven insights effectively.

Foster a Culture of Innovation
- Upskill employees to embrace AI confidently and competently.
- Recognize and reward individuals who leverage AI creatively to solve business challenges.

Establish Ethical Guardrails
- Implement policies that address fairness, transparency and accountability in AI use.
- Stay informed about regulatory frameworks, ensuring compliance across markets.

Iterate and Improve Continuously
- Monitor AI systems regularly to assess their performance and relevance.
- Stay ahead of advancements, adapting systems to maintain competitive advantages.

Key Takeaways for CEOs

Embrace AI as a Partner: Use AI to enhance -- not replace -- human decision-making, allowing technology and intuition to work harmoniously.

Data Drives Success: Prioritize data quality and governance to ensure AI delivers meaningful, unbiased insights.

> **Lead the Charge:** Inspire confidence and engagement by championing AI adoption across the organization.
>
> **Think Big, Start Smart:** Begin with manageable pilot projects, scaling success into enterprise-wide impact.
>
> **Stay Ethical and Transparent:** Maintain transparency, fairness, and accountability in AI applications to build trust with stakeholders.

AI is more than a tool -- it's a mindset and a strategic differentiator. By integrating AI thoughtfully and strategically, leaders can build their organizations with smarter decisions, greater resilience and lasting success.

Chapter 20

Balancing Creativity and Execution:

Leadership in Structure, Experimentation and Results

Exceptional leaders understand this fundamental truth: Vision ignites, but execution transforms.

Leadership, particularly the leadership required to balance vision and execution, is crucial for cultivating an environment where big ideas flourish and tangible results are delivered. This delicate balance is the linchpin of innovation and operational excellence which are the dual engines driving long-term growth and competitive advantage.

This chapter explores actionable strategies for balancing creativity with execution. Learn how to build frameworks that support experimentation within reason, nurture discipline and produce outcomes that resonate across teams, stakeholders and markets.

The Power of Balancing Creativity and Execution

There are many reasons leaders spend time trying to identify the best ways to balance creativity and execution. Creativity without execution is potentially futile at best and dangerous at worst.

Creativity isn't a luxury -- it's your organization's lifeblood. It propels new products, business models, and fresh solutions that position your company as an industry leader. Dynamic cultures of creativity attract the best minds. Talented professionals want to contribute to environments where ideas ignite action.

Vision coupled with creativity but without execution is just a dream. Turning ideas into action builds trust with employees which reverberates to customers and stakeholders. Being on top of execution is a testament to your leadership and the hard work of your team: Execution is the tangible result of your shared vision. Strong execution demonstrates reliability, creating a foundation of credibility while confirming you are a leader who supports growth and takes calculated risks.

Remember: Creativity Fuels Innovation. Execution Delivers Results.

Principles for Mastering the Balance

The sweet spot is balance. Here's why: Too much creativity? Chaos and inefficiency reign. Too much execution? Innovation stalls and opportunities fade. The magic is in the harmony -- where ideas meet disciplined action. So how do leaders do it? They define their vision in a way that inspires and guides with the following strategies:

- **Outline Big Picture Goals**: Set audacious, inspiring objectives that spark bold thinking.
- **Define Tactical Pathways**: Ground your vision in detailed roadmaps, ensuring every innovative idea has a clear execution path.

- **Demand A Culture of Experimentation and Accountability**: This is not just about taking risks, but about taking risks with intention. Empower teams to explore new ideas, while ensuring that this experimentation is aligned with overarching goals. This is the kind of culture that fosters creativity without derailing focus.
- **Encourage Risk with Intention**: Empower teams to explore new ideas while aligning experimentation with overarching goals.
- **Connect Responsibility and Ownership with the Outcomes**: Instill a sense of responsibility for delivering results while celebrating the learning journey.

To truly create a dream team of innovators, you'll need to bring together imaginative visionaries and practical implementers. This combination of personality traits and skills will help resilience and ingenuity to excel. Simultaneously, foster collaboration across creative and operational functions to ensure alignment and shared ownership. Lastly, encourage feedback-driven improvement, every step of the way, while blending flexibility with disciplined refinement. Staying nimble will help because you may need to pivot with purpose when new insights or challenges arise.

Strategies for Leading the Balance

Whenever you're trying to accelerate your company's growth by innovating – keeping energy, time, financial commitments and teams balanced will be essential. Smart leaders accomplish this by doing the following:

> **Define Frameworks for Freedom and Structure that Elevates, Not Stifles.** To give the latitude necessary for innovation, insist on plans and updates that utilize methodologies that identify objectives and key results (OKRs) to provide clarity without hampering creativity.
>
> **Aim for Consistency Without Rigidity**: Processes and tools should streamline, not restrain, innovation and execution.

Practice Experimentation with Purpose: Set boundaries for experimentation such as budget limits, timelines and/or strategic alignments so creativity doesn't derail focus.

Encourage Quick Wins, Big Learnings: Prototype rapidly and embrace the insights from every iteration.

Identify Metrics that Matter: Track innovation alongside operational outcomes. Celebrate both.

Reward the Spectrum: Recognize contributions across all process stages, from ideation to flawless delivery.

Your leadership role is to be both visionary and action-oriented. Your team will follow your example. Your actions set the tone for the entire organization, demonstrating the balance you seek and inspiring others to follow suit.

Case Study: The Future Technologies Inc. Transformation

Background:

FutureTechnologies, a technology leader, faced a disconnect between creativity and execution. Visionaries felt shackled by process, while execution teams needed help with unclear priorities. Further, the marketing and tech execution teams were in a state of ongoing conflict.

To create alignment, the following actions were taken.

Innovation Sprints: Clear objectives and timelines were demanded while creativity was encouraged within structured boundaries.

Agile Execution: Streamlined workflows were identified and implemented to ensure operational efficiency without sacrificing flexibility.

Collaboration in Action: Cross-functional "innovation reviews" aligned teams and clarified priorities. The creative "imaginers" were paired with the tech building "engineers." Marketing leaders were introduced to developments before their completion so they could begin visualizing future launch plans.

Balanced Metrics: KPIs were tracked, including idea-to-market speed, revenue from innovation, and operational consistency.

Outcome: Launch times got about 30% faster, market share began improving and employee engagement soared. FutureTechnologies' ability to innovate and execute in harmony became its defining competitive edge.

Obstacles & Solutions for Balancing Challenges Between Creativity and Action

Let's review some of the resistance leaders may encounter when trying to balance creative juices with actionable energies.

Resistance to Change

Obstacle: Shifting toward balance disrupts routines.

Solution: Communicate the why and involve teams in shaping the path forward.

Misaligned Priorities

Obstacle: Creative and execution teams often work in silos.

Solution: Build alignment through shared frameworks, frequent communication, and mutual respect.

Fear of Failure

Obstacle: Risk-averse teams limit potential.

Solution: Celebrate learning. Highlight how failures often pave the way for the greatest successes. Set boundaries so the failures are contained both cost and impact-wise.

Leadership Takeaways

Those who lead boldly and push for mergers between creativity and action build a variety of benefits for their companies. These get down to a few of the following.

> **Visionary Action Wins**: Pairing your boldest ideas with precise execution can help you outpace the competition.
>
> **Structure Fuels Innovation**: The right frameworks encourage freedom within purpose-driven boundaries.
>
> **Experimentation Pays Off**: If you don't try, you know pretty much what you'll get – and it won't be anything new. Calculated risks lead to breakthroughs. Lean into them.
>
> **Dynamic Balance**: Continuously assess and recalibrate to meet changing market needs.
>
> **Leadership Inspires**: As the leader of your company, organization, or department -- embody the balance you wish to see. Your team will rise to meet your example.

Mastering the balance between creativity and execution isn't just a leadership skill -- it's a legacy. When leaders inspire their teams with structure while encouraging experimentation and prioritizing results, they create more than a business -- they build an enduring force of innovation and impact. Let the balance you strike today shape the success of tomorrow.

Section V
People and Culture

Chapter 21

Future-Proofing the Workforce:

The Leadership Role in HR Strategy and Resilience

The world moves fast -- and today it is moving faster than ever before. Technology evolves overnight, markets shift unpredictably, and global challenges continue to rewrite the rules of engagement. In this ever-changing landscape, your workforce isn't just a resource; it's the heartbeat of your business -- the driver of innovation, adaptability and growth.

As a CEO, you hold the reins of this powerful force. Your ability to anticipate, plan and lead in shaping the workforce of tomorrow is more than a strategy; it's a mandate for long-term resilience and success. Future-proofing your workforce isn't just about surviving disruption -- it's about thriving in its midst.

This chapter empowers you to take bold steps toward creating an adaptable, innovative and competitive workforce by focusing on forward-thinking HR strategies.

The Imperative for Future-Proofing the Workforce

Let's begin with navigating technological disruption:

- Automation, AI, and digital transformation are redefining industries as we discussed in the prior chapter. As a forward-thinking leader, you understand that your team needs the tools and training to evolve alongside these rapid changes. By investing in education and empowerment, you're not just ensuring survival; you're leading the way. Invest in education and empowerment. A tech-savvy workforce doesn't just survive; it leads.

You'll need to win over the best talent:

- Certain fields like cybersecurity, data science, and renewable energy are fiercely competitive. As a leader, you know that a future-ready team will continue to attract additional top-quality talent and ultimately best position your organization for growth. Be the leader who offers more than a job: Provide a future of opportunities and watch your organization thrive.

Building resilience during uncertainty is a constant:

- Crises are omnipresent and they are constant tests for organizations. However, a workforce with flexibility and cross-functional skills will be better able to transform these tests into triumphs.
- Resilience starts at the top. As a visionary leader if you focus on the importance of flexibility and adaptability, your team will follow your lead. Your influence is key in shaping a workforce that can transform global crises into triumphs.

Leadership Strategies for Workforce Development

Great leaders are constantly on the lookout for the best talent they can afford. But it doesn't stop with "the hire." Employees need to have their talents raised for any company to remain viable. Strategies to develop the best workforce you can, include:

> **Upskilling & Reskilling for the Long Game.** Foster a culture of perpetual learning. Knowledge isn't static; neither is success. Partner with educational institutions and leverage online platforms to provide certification programs that align with emerging trends.
>
> **Embrace Flexible Work Models.** Adaptability isn't a buzzword -- it's a necessity. Hybrid models, global talent access, and training for non-traditional work environments ensure your workforce thrives in any situation.
>
> **Plan for Tomorrow, Today.** Leadership pipelines don't build themselves. Nurture your future leaders with cross-functional exposure and robust mentorship programs. Stability and succession are the cornerstones of organizational longevity.
>
> **Prioritize Well-Being.** A healthy workforce is a productive one. Commit to wellness initiatives that address physical, mental and financial health. Balance isn't just a goal -- it's a strategy for reducing burnout and enhancing creativity.
>
> **Champion Diversity & Inclusion.** Bias has no place in future-forward hiring. Hire the best people you can, offer training and position all employees for success. Diversity isn't just a metric; it holds the potential to be an engine of innovation as you gather input from all kinds of people with a variety of cultural and life experiences that may contribute to understanding and opening new market opportunities.

Be the Catalyst: The best leaders know their role is to...

Set the Vision: Define the "why" behind your strategy and share it boldly. Inspire your team and stakeholders by aligning HR initiatives with organizational goals.

Allocate Resources: Put your money where your mission is. Budget for growth, invest in tech and ensure your workforce has the tools to succeed.

Champion the Culture: Growth starts at the top. When you lead by example -- prioritizing adaptability and celebrating wins -- you pave the way for a resilient, innovative organization.

▪ *Action Steps for Building an Agile Workforce*

Someone said, "When it comes to your employees, you'll get what you inspect but not necessarily what you expect." What a great lesson to remember. Smart leaders elevate inspection results by incorporating these 4 steps whenever possible.

> **Conduct Skills Audits: These are used to** identify the strengths and gaps of your workforce. Skill audits help to anticipate tomorrow's needs today.
>
> **Design Tailored Training Programs:** Define and offer personalized learning opportunities, blending workshops, e-learning, and practical applications. These can be outside of your organization. Most employees appreciate ongoing learning opportunities and earning certificates within their sectors and roles.
>
> **Create Flexibility with Intention:** Embrace job rotation, project-based work, and gig talent to foster a dynamic, versatile team. Whenever possible have employees experience what others do during their days. This builds not only a greater understanding of how the company functions, but also builds empathy for the challenges others deal with throughout their days.
>
> **Measure & Refine:** Regularly review employee feedback and performance metrics to ensure your strategies are delivering the results you seek. Adjust course when needed.

The Takeaway

Your workforce is your legacy. By championing continuous learning, adaptability and resilience, you are safeguarding your organization and empowering your people to fulfill a mission they can be proud to be a part of. Lead boldly. Inspire relentlessly. The future is yours to build -- one step, one strategy, one inspired team at a time.

Chapter 22

Corporate Culture as a Growth Strategy:

Igniting Success with Purpose and Passion

Corporate culture isn't a buzzword or a nice-to-have. It's the transformative power that can shape the soul of your business. It influences how your employees show up, how your customers feel, and how the world views your brand. For CEOs, embracing and defining culture isn't just a leadership duty -- it's a powerful growth strategy that can ignite success with purpose and passion.

When culture is purposefully crafted and authentically lived, it ignites passion, aligns teams and fuels success that transcends profits: It's a big component of creating networks that reach far and wide. This chapter dives deep into why culture matters and how you, as the Boss, can champion it as a driving force for sustained growth, resilience and market leadership. Your role is not just significant, it's indispensable.

The Power of Culture

There are many reasons why you want to create a corporate culture that reflects your leadership personality, style and vision for the ultimate direction of your company. Let's look at several benefits of cultural leadership.

A company that defines its culture in a meaningful way...

Drives Employee Engagement and Retention

- **Purpose Fuels Passion**: Employees thrive in cultures where they feel seen, valued and aligned with the mission. Purpose-driven teams aren't just productive -- they understand the mission and as such become unstoppable.
- **Retention Superpower**: A culture that resonates from the top down and through every department keeps your talent grounded, loyal and inspired to grow with you.

Enhances Brand Reputation

- **Magnetic Presence**: Companies with strong cultures attract customers who see themselves in your values. Connection drives loyalty in a plethora of ways.
- **Employer of Choice**: A great workplace isn't just about perks -- it's about people. You can have a great physical office but a toxic workplace. A respected culture pulls in top talent effortlessly and solidifies an uplifting spirit of camaraderie and teamwork.

Aligns Organizational Goals

- **Unified Decision-Making**: A shared cultural framework establishes the potential to make decision-making a bit more streamlined and consistent.
- **Collaborative Energy**: When teams are aligned in values – siloed thinking breaks down which in turn gasses up creativity and accelerates momentum.

Supports Adaptability and Resilience

- **Change with Confidence**: In uncertain times, culture is a guiding star. It can be the difference that inspires employees to navigate disruption with clarity and strength – versus jumping ship when the going gets rough and all hands are needed on deck.
- **Crisis-Proof**: A united, values-driven workforce reacts to challenges with agility and determination.

Fuels Business Performance

- **Customer Love**: Customers feel it when employees like and live by the values of the company. The result? Employees are inspired to provide exceptional customer experiences that drive loyalty.
- **Profit Amplifier**: Companies with strong cultures consistently outperform competitors, delivering market-leading results.

Building Your Culture: Define It, Live It

So, the benefits of creating a unifying culture are clear, but how can you do it authentically and effectively? Here are some of the best considerations.

Define Core Values That Matter

- **Find Your North Star**: It starts at the top: You're the leader so you must decide why you're doing what you do. What's the value? Why is it important? Then, with your vision defined, set your action plan while also seeking opinions and input from others. Collaborate with your leadership team and employees to identify values that reflect the true corporate identity you envision.
- **Stay Authentic**: Keep it simple and direct. Skip the fluff. Define values that are actionable and resonate across the organization.

Articulate a Vision That Inspires

- **Write a Culture Manifesto**: Share your vision in a compelling way that connects hearts and minds. This might take some time, but consider it your Constitution: An important, guiding, living and breathing document that has an amendable process built-in, if necessary.
- **Get Leadership Commitment**: Your supporting leadership team must join you to champion your stated vision. Everyone needs to be living it in every decision and interaction.

Bring Employees on the Journey

- **Encourage Collaborative Creation**: Involve your teams in shaping cultural initiatives. Your employees are not just the order-taking contingent of the corporate culture you seek to create, they are the heart of it. Their input and involvement are always going to be crucial to the success of your culture which equates to the success of your company.
- **Feedback as Fuel**: Regularly gather employee input to ensure your culture evolves with their needs and aspirations. Just like you change – employees change, industries change, environments change, attitudes change, demands change – and so it goes on a daily basis. Regular pulse checks keep companies and the hearts of their cultures beating in healthy ways.

Bringing Culture to Life

Once you envision the corporate culture you desire and define it, you'll need to set the stage to truly live it. Here are some of the best ways to make an exciting culture of success a reality.

Lead with Actions, Not Words

- **Be the Example**: Your actions set the standard. Demonstrate your commitment through visible, impactful decisions.
- **Invest in Priorities**: Fund initiatives that bring your culture to life.

Hire for Values and Growth

- **Align for Fit**: Skills can be taught; values are foundational. Recruit individuals who embody your company's ethos.
- **Celebrate Diversity**: Build a culture enriched by unique perspectives and backgrounds.

Immerse New Talent in Culture

- **Use Onboarding as Inspiration**: Use the onboarding process to immerse new hires in the company's values, vision and community.
- **Treat Mentorship as a Bridge**: Pair new hires with culture ambassadors who live and breathe the organization's ethos.

Reinforce Through Everyday Practices

- **Reward What Matters**: Recognize and celebrate employees who exemplify the culture in action. The recognition can be simple, even humorous, yet still effective: I know of a CEO who rewarded the "Employee of the Week" with a banana. Yes, for a week they were the Top Banana. To my surprise, this was a coveted title and one held in great esteem because it was positioned to be the ultimate honor for work well done during that prior week.
- **Use an Assortment of Communication Tools as a Catalyst**: Regularly highlight wins and initiatives through all communication channels.

Continuously Evolve

- **Measure What You Value**: Regularly assess engagement and alignment to keep your culture vibrant.
- **Adapt to Thrive**: Stay ahead by evolving your culture to meet new challenges and opportunities.

The Competitive Edge of Culture

IF you happen to still be doubting the paramount nature of establishing a corporate culture, let's look at how it adds to your competitive edge.

A solidly defined corporate culture is your....

> **Talent Magnet**: Your culture isn't just a set of words -- it's your superpower in attracting and retaining talent. People want to belong to something meaningful.
>
> **Market Differentiator**: A company with values-driven innovation and customer connection doesn't just compete -- it dominates.
>
> **Scaffold for Scalable Growth**: Strong cultures grow with you, creating cohesion across teams, departments and geographies.

The Leader's Playbook Recap

As you define your culture and commit to setting it as the way forward, keep the following ideas top of mind.

> **Culture IS Strategy**: Build it deliberately, and your business will thrive.
>
> **Lead with Purpose**: Your authenticity sets the tone.
>
> **Involve Everyone**: When employees own the culture, it flourishes.
>
> **Measure, Adapt, Grow**: Keep refining for continuous improvement.

When corporate culture is treated as the powerful growth engine it is, the results ripple outward. You create more than a business -- you define a legacy. A strong, aligned culture doesn't just declare who you are as a company today; it propels you and your company into the future by inspiring employees, customers and even investors to join your journey.

Chapter 23

Diversity, Equity, and Inclusion:

Unlocking the Power of People and Purpose

*L**et me say this right up front: I'm a fan of excellence and merit. From my perspective, those who deliver for a company by bringing their talent and sharing it to the max are of utmost importance. Time and time again – I've seen excellence delivered by people coming from every color of the rainbow. In doing so, they earned their rewards. Most times, it was because their commitment to excellence was a continual force driving them. My companies and clients were the lucky recipients of their talents and commitment to excel. They were recognized and rewarded for this, both via their elevated personal pride and financial status. At the time of the printing of this book, the phrases "Diversity, Equity, and Inclusion (DEI)" – pushed to the point of trying to replace merit and excellence – are still being debated for what they mean. Some will say DEI is no longer optional -- the three together are the key to unlocking your organization's potential. I do not wholly agree with this: If I'm getting on a jetliner – I want the best pilot, the most experienced pilot, the calm-under-pressure pilot. I can say the same if I'm ever stuck in a burning building: If the firefighter has more guts than most and the physical stamina and ability to get me and others out of a burning building,* *potentially – and bravely – carrying the unconscious – that's the firefighter I want on the Fire Department trucks. While the concept of DEI is touted to fuel innovation while creating a culture where every employee can thrive – these are words in a vacuum: When any member of a team does not pull their weight, when they are not up to par for the task, when others have to carry their load – they are a detriment to an organization and quite possibly society-at-large, as well as maybe even lives. As the saying goes: We cannot put square pegs into round holes. Every person has their skill set. If anything, I believe it is beneficial to society, to be honest about this and to help people find the roles that complement their talents as we train those willing to learn.*

Consider this chapter as an acknowledgment of DEI and find ways to leverage it as a growth strategy. The idea is to see that it doesn't just align with your business goals but ideally finds ways to propel them forward.

Making the Case for DEI

Let's break down these three concepts: diversity, equity and inclusion.

Diversity is defined as... the presence of differences within a group, organization, or society, encompassing various dimensions such as race, ethnicity, gender, age, sexual orientation, ability, socioeconomic status, religion, and more.

Equity is defined as... fair and just treatment of individuals by recognizing and addressing systemic inequalities and providing opportunities and resources based on individual needs to ensure everyone has access to the same outcomes.

Inclusion is defined as... the intentional creation of environments where all individuals feel valued, respected, supported, and empowered to fully participate and contribute, fostering a sense of belonging for everyone.

Now on first read, those do sound like good ideas. That said, critics argue that there is a big issue if identity – anyone's – is prioritized over competence or that a demographic criterion is the goal vs. merit. There's also a belief that DEI reverse discriminates. Politics enter the picture as well, raising the question of whether the hire is for appearance or compliance rather than substantive change or true inclusion. Certainly, there are plenty of areas where DEI efforts could lead to division rather than unity – which is counter to a successful culture and company.

So, how do leaders counter the tensions between the good intentions of DEI to promote fairness and the practical implications – or even more so, the perceptions – of how these initiatives are implemented? In this chapter, we'll look at this.

Let's examine some important principles for integrating a DEI strategy.

> **Focus on Authenticity Over Optics**: Move beyond surface-level efforts to drive meaningful, lasting change.
>
> **Accountability Matters**: Tie executive performance metrics directly to DEI outcomes.
>
> **Pipeline Development**: Invest in programs that nurture underrepresented talent for future leadership roles.
>
> **Establish Baseline Metrics**: Assess your company's current state of diversity across your workforce.
>
> **Be transparent Progress**: Share measurable goals and outcomes with employees, investors and stakeholders.
>
> **Inclusive Hiring**: Consider "blind" first interviews to eliminate bias in recruitment and proactively seek diverse talent pools.
>
> **Encourage Proposals from a Variety of Suppliers**: Allow a broad range of suppliers to submit bids for your business.

Community Engagement: Partner with organizations that support underrepresented communities.

Advocacy Leadership: Use your corporate platform to advocate for equity and inclusion across industries.

Merit and excellence are foundational to fostering growth, innovation and success. They underscore the importance of recognizing and rewarding the talent, effort, and achievement of employees. When these principles are thoughtfully blended with diversity, equity and inclusion (DEI) initiatives, they ensure that equal opportunities are accessible to a broad spectrum of individuals, regardless of their backgrounds. This alignment is crucial in creating an environment where diverse talents thrive because a culture has been defined that values individual contributions and collective advancement. This synergy enhances fairness and drives sustainable excellence by leveraging the strengths of diverse perspectives.

Chapter 24

Retaining Top Talent:

Leadership Strategies to Build Loyalty and Drive Excellence

In today's fast-paced, talent-driven world, the value of retaining top performers cannot be overstated. They are not just a strategy, but your competitive edge. High achievers bring unparalleled creativity, expertise and leadership potential. They're the driving force behind innovation and excellence. But in an era where career mobility is the norm and workplace expectations are evolving, retaining the best of the best requires more than a paycheck.
It demands authentic leadership, a clear vision, and a culture where people can thrive.

This chapter unpacks actionable strategies to inspire loyalty and ensure your organization remains a destination for exceptional talent, showing the powerful impact of your leadership on loyalty.

The Value of Retaining Top Talent

If you doubt the importance of retaining your top talent, let's take a look at why this is short-sighted thinking.

Retaining your top talent…

> **Helps to protect institutional knowledge.** When your top performers leave, they take with them critical expertise and relationships that fuel success. This loss can disrupt momentum and team dynamics, leading to a significant setback in your business operations and growth.
>
> **Are often performance drivers.** High achievers are more likely to deliver results, spark innovation, and enhance your organization's market reputation.
>
> **Is a cost-efficiency strategy.** Replacing employees is expensive. Retention protects your investment in recruitment, training and onboarding.
>
> **Builds your employer brand becoming a magnet for talent.** Retaining top talent reinforces your reputation as a great workplace, making it easier to attract future stars.

Leadership Insights for Inspiring Loyalty

Let's look at a variety of ways leaders inspire the loyalty of their best employees.

The best leaders…

> **Lead with Authenticity and Integrity:** They transparently share their vision and challenges openly while their actions align with their words. This honesty helps to earn trust.

Create a Vision Employees Believe In: They inspire action by creating a bold and compelling vision that is achievable. This excites employees to join the journey.

Engage Talent: They involve their top performers in shaping and defining the strategy and key initiatives. By sharing a sense of ownership, buy-in is achieved.

Celebrate and Reward Contributions: They understand the power of public acknowledgment of achievements through awards, team shout-outs, and/or personal notes. Additionally, they tailor incentives -- whether bonuses, professional development, and/or time off -- to individual preferences.

Prioritize Growth and Development: They offer employees opportunities to tackle roles that challenge and expand their skill sets. In the process, they invest in training and mentorship to prepare team members for future opportunities.

Foster a Thriving Culture: Leaders build teams that emphasize respect, inclusivity and camaraderie. At the same time, they encourage flexibility to prevent burnout and promote well-being.

Empower with Autonomy: Leaders who choose their team members carefully, have greater confidence in allowing their employees to make decisions and lead initiatives. They encourage them to reach but holler for help before they might stumble. Further, great leaders provide resources and guidance yet do their best to avoid micromanagement.

Traits of Leaders Who Inspire Loyalty

Being a leader means you have to develop the skills that inspire loyalty. Here are a few of them for your consideration.

Inspire Boldly: Paint a future that employees are excited to be part of.

Stay Positive: Confidence and optimism energize teams, even during challenges.

Empower Others: Focus on supporting your employees' success and growth.

Lead by Example: Show humility and be willing to get hands-on when needed.

Flexibility Wins: Encourage experimentation and adapt to changing needs.

Be Feedback-Friendly: Listen, learn, and adjust your approach to meet your team's expectations.

Promote Belonging: Ensure every team member feels valued and respected.

Fairness First: Recognize and mitigate biases to promote equity.

Keep in mind that people are different (in every sense of the word.) While you are trying to run your business, a one-size-fits-all approach may not be the best way to motivate and get the best work from everyone. Smart leaders set the stage, find the best players for each role and encourage them to perform – while offering skills development and support. Companies that do this tend to secure the best of the best.

Key Takeaways for Leaders

To wrap up this chapter, let's close with four key take-aways.

Leadership Drives Retention: Be the role model your employees aspire to follow.

Growth Keeps Talent Engaged: Offer opportunities that challenge and excite.

Promote Genuine Connection: Build relationships that make employees feel valued and empowered.

Adapt to Succeed: Continuously evolve your retention strategies to meet changing workforce needs.

Retention isn't just about keeping great people -- it's about building a workplace where they can thrive, innovate and lead. In today's competitive landscape, prioritizing top talent retention is more than a strategy -- it's your leadership legacy.

Chapter 25

Leading in a Hybrid Work World:

Balancing Flexibility and Accountability for Maximum Impact

In the early 2020s, hybrid work became more than just a trend: For some businesses, it's now the new reality. Certainly, there are both plusses and minuses of hybrid work structures. Not every business can offer hybrid work. Further, not all roles within a company are adaptable to hybrid work – and this in itself is a very serious leadership challenge considering the inequities and divisiveness this may create.

While the hybrid model, where employees work remotely at home and also in the office, offers benefits for some, such as greater flexibility, access to broader talent pools and reduced costs -- it also presents real challenges for business leaders starting with maintaining accountability, fostering collaboration, developing a workforce for the future and preserving organizational culture – to just name a few.

As a leader, you may benefit by finding ways to make hybrid work not just as a logistical adjustment – but as a strategic advantage. You also may find that hybrid working is simply not the way you want to run your company. This chapter shares some insights and strategies for balancing flexibility with accountability to create a thriving hybrid workforce that drives innovation and engagement if this is the work structure you choose to adopt.

The Argument for Hybrid Work Schedules

There are multiple considerations when assessing the advantages and disadvantages of hybrid work scheduling. Let's look at both.

The Possible Pros

- Employees increasingly value the freedom to manage their time, seamlessly blending work and life responsibilities.
- Hybrid work helps employees achieve work-life harmony, increasing satisfaction and retention.
- Talent possibilities may expand if you can tap into a global talent pool, bringing diverse perspectives and expertise to your organization.
- You might be able to access new employees from pools of people such as caregivers or individuals with disabilities.
- Many employees report being more focused and productive when given the flexibility of hybrid work.
- There may be financial benefits such as reduced cost of office space and overhead, freeing up resources for other strategic investments.

The Possible Cons

- Remote employees may feel their contributions are less recognized when compared to in-office peers.
- Work standards might be trickier to define and assess, leading to inconsistency across teams, which may ultimately create confusion and add to inequities.

- Collaboration and culture may weaken and hinder innovation due to a lack of regular face-to-face interactions that may otherwise strengthen relationships.
- Remote employees risk feeling isolated from the company's mission and values.
- Remote employees may miss out on networking and development opportunities.
- Unequal access to reliable technology tools and resources can exacerbate a digital divide.

Principles for Hybrid Work Success

If you are thinking about keeping a hybrid work model as part of your business plan, here are principles to consider for success.

- Outline clear guidelines for eligibility, expectations, and communication protocols.
- Allow departments to tailor hybrid work practices to their needs while maintaining consistency.
- Ensure equal access to resources and opportunities for all employees, regardless of location.
- Regularly evaluate hybrid policies to identify and address any unintended inequities. Monitor work carefully. You'll get what you inspect not necessarily what you expect.
- Focus on prioritizing deliverables. Shift from measuring hours to assessing results. Use metrics like productivity, engagement and retention to assess the impact of hybrid work.
- Maintain regular communication to ensure alignment and support. Insist on check-ins.
- Schedule team gatherings and collaborative days to strengthen relationships.
- Use technology to develop a sense of belonging through virtual activities and recognition programs.
- Designate specific days for team collaboration in the office.
- As the leader, be visible and accessible to both remote and in-office employees.

- Equip your managers with the skills to manage hybrid teams equitably and effectively.
- Create feedback loops to refine hybrid policies based on employee input.
- Consider productivity tracking software if you provide corporate computers.

Hybrid work is going to be debated for years to come. Some leaders will put the kibosh on it for a variety of very good reasons, others may decide it fits their work models and benefits their budgets. It's a free market economy: Employees and Employers will continue to "find the best fits."

Section VI

Communication and Influence

Chapter 26

Media Relations in the Digital Age:

Mastering the Art of Shaping Public Perception with Visionary Leadership

Media relations has evolved into a dynamic and multi-faceted discipline in today's hyper-connected world. Leaders no longer manage traditional press interactions alone -- they must now also navigate the complexities of social media, online influencers, and a relentless 24/7 news cycle.

Effective media relations are about way more than controlling narratives; it's about building trust while amplifying your company's mission and safeguarding its reputation in an era where information -- and misinformation -- can spread in seconds.

This chapter aims to equip you with a good understanding of the tools at your disposal to harness the power of media strategically and responsibly, ensuring you are better able to lead your organization and the conversation, even during challenging times.

The Power of Media Relations

The media – newspapers, magazines, radio, cable and traditional TV along with digital outlets and social media – offer plenty of opportunities to promote yourself, your team and your corporate goods, services and agenda if you know how to engage with each vertical to your benefit.

Let's explore the power of media relations and why you want to learn how to best use it for your benefit.

> **Amplifying Your Vision:** Media relations help broadcast your company's achievements, mission, and values to audiences across traditional and digital platforms. Proactive engagement ensures your story remains consistent, resonant, and impactful.
>
> **Building Trust and Credibility:** Thoughtful media engagement positions you and your organization as credible, trustworthy, and forward-thinking. Strong media relationships fortify trust with investors, customers, and communities.
>
> **Navigating Crises with Confidence:** Swift, strategic communication planning mitigates speculation and minimizes reputational damage, putting you in control of the narrative. In a digital-first world, media relations can neutralize false narratives before they take root.

Core Elements of Modern Media Relations

There are a variety of elements that are relevant to a solid media relations plan.

- **Press Releases that Pop**: Keep your press releases concise, compelling, informative and newsworthy to capture journalists' attention.
- **Executive Insights**: A good media relations strategy positions your leadership team as go-to experts for industry commentary and thought leadership opining.
- **Relationships Matter**: Building authentic, trust-based connections with journalists and editors is paramount. Work on establishing these relationships daily and do so before you might need a "friendly" outlet in the event of a crisis.
- **Social Media Is Your Megaphone**: Depending on your industry – any of the platforms from LinkedIn to X to Instagram to Facebook to Pinterest and many others enable direct, authentic engagement with your audiences. Explore them all and find your tribe.
- **Influencer Partnerships**: Collaborating with digital thought leaders to expand your reach and credibility is a strategy for a lot of industries. Can you take advantage of this potential?
- **Own Your Story**: Company blogs, podcasts, and videos all allow you to define your narrative on your terms. Explore and experiment with all of these media formats.
- **Always Be Monitoring**: Use tools like Google Alerts, Hootsuite, or any of the advanced social listening platforms to stay ahead of mentions and sentiment shifts.
- **Craft Swift, Unified Responses**: Pre-approved messaging frameworks ensure speed and consistency in addressing crises. Define who gets to stay what, when and how.
- **Transparency Wins**: In difficult times, remember this: Honesty and authenticity strengthen trust and loyalty. Don't make people detectives because you are avoiding being direct. They will find whatever they're looking for – or will cast enough doubt with others, believing that they found "something" that puts you on trial in the Court of Public Opinion.

Shaping Public Perception

Smart leaders take full advantage of shaping the public's perceptions and perspectives using the media. Remember, the public includes partners, customers, shareholders, stakeholders, regulators, employees and others.

To craft a compelling narrative and position yourself as an industry thought leader, you'll want to carefully contemplate the following:

- **Know Your Core Story**: Clearly define the values, mission and vision you want to communicate about your company and yourself as its leader.
- **Tailor for Impact**: You will have to adapt your messaging to resonate with different media outlets as well as with stakeholders, from investors to employees. A trade publication might appreciate the intricacies of how you manage an industry-wide challenge. However, a national news outlet is more likely interested in your leadership vision and possibly your financial statements!
- **Consistency is Key**: Ensure every channel -- press, social media, internal communications -- reinforces the same story. Remember, anything and everything -- whether said or put in writing – can get on the internet for the world to see and read. Be consistent. Ask, for example: Would I want my competitors to see this? How will my clients feel?
- **Offer Insightful Commentary**: Be prepared to share bold perspectives on industry trends through op-eds, news interviews, contributed articles, podcasts, and/or panel discussions, etc.
- **Humanize Your Leadership Team**: For yourself and other managers, use personal stories to forge deeper emotional connections with audiences. Behind every business is a person who is imagineering, inspiring, defining and leading the way.
- **Remember Visibility Matters**: Be present and engaged across media platforms to reinforce credibility and authority.

- **Empowering Your Team**: Invest in media training for yourself and other key executives so they are better able to confidently handle interviews and public appearances.
- **Stay Proactive**: Regularly share updates with the media to stay relevant and top-of-mind. Don't be afraid if you have to share a less-than-positive update. If you've been consistent with sharing all of your developments, they might go for the headline – but it may also be somewhat softened because they have witnessed your consistency and leadership style in the past.
- **Balance the Mix**: Integrate traditional outreach with innovative digital campaigns to maximize your reach.

Tackling Media Challenges in the Digital Era

There are a variety of challenges confronting every leader in this digital age where citizen journalism is literally "taking the front page." Let's look at a few of the potential challenges, opportunities and actionable steps you'll want to consider.

> **Misinformation**: False narratives can spread rapidly, eroding trust in their wake. You will need to have a plan – or at least the outline of one. Since every crisis is different and rarely predictable, you'll want to stay on the go, ready to respond swiftly to correct inaccuracies decisively and use your owned media platforms to further clarify and reiterate the facts.
>
> **Platform Overload**: There are a lot of media channels and the sheer volume of them all can dilute your message. However, maybe not. The people who get their news from X are not necessarily the same as those who go to LinkedIn, Instagram, Facebook or Reddit, for example. Consider conducting a pros and cons analysis of each platform and decide which one(s) are most aligned with your public audience.
>
> **Balancing Transparency with Sensitivity**: Being too open may risk exposing vulnerabilities while withholding erodes trust. If you are leading a public company, depending on the news development, you may not have an option for disclosure.

Further, there could be a clock that starts to tick if the issue is "material information" – defining the exact amount of time you have to get that disclosure ready for mass distribution and consumption. In light of all this, you'll want to create and follow a consistent plan for issuing news that impacts shareholders and stakeholders, while protecting sensitive information, as necessary.

Build a Media Toolkit: Prepare yourself for media opportunities by assembling a comprehensive press kit with company facts, executive bios, and visually engaging materials. Keep it up to date! Include the best photos, videos and imagery that you can – after all, you may see it on the front page of a major outlet one day!

Talking Points Matter: Develop concise, consistent answers to frequently asked questions. Practice saying them like a Broadway Star – not like a robot.

Engage Authentically: Use social media to share insights, connect with stakeholders, and humanize your leadership. It's ok and even good to throw in some personality… you are a person, right?

Be Visible on LinkedIn: LinkedIn is the status-quo site that others in business will visit to check you out. Use this platform to establish your presence as a credible leader, sharing ideas that spark dialogue and innovation. Likewise share content from others and comment on their posts that are relevant to your company and/or industry, as well.

Anticipate Risks: Identify vulnerabilities and prepare tailored crisis response plans. Work with a perception analyst, your investment banking advisory team and/or other experts to help you objectively assess all the facts and subjective issues that will arise.

Assign Roles: Empower a crisis response team to act decisively when/if needed. Did I mention hiring experts? It may be the best money you ever spent for a variety of reasons – including their emotions will be a level removed from those directly employed at the company and also they've likely been hired to deal with many crises (good, bad and neutral) so they'll bring more the necessary experience and calm.

Monitor Impact: Use analytics to measure media coverage, social media engagement and public sentiment. Ask customers "How did you hear about us?" "Do you follow our social media feeds?" Perception audits can be very helpful for gathering this kind of information.

Adapt to Win: Regularly evaluate and adjust your media strategy to stay ahead of emerging trends.

Key Insights for Mastering Media Relations

In closing this chapter, there are 6 Key Points you'll want to keep in mind when it comes to mastering media relations.

Own the Narrative: Define your story, control the messaging, and ensure platform consistency because if you don't, someone else will. In public relations, the best strategy is offensive, defensive is never the first choice – and it doesn't have to be.

Harness the Power of Digital: Leverage social media and owned platforms like your corporate website to connect directly with stakeholders and also be a repository of relevant corporate information. This should include information about products as well as bios of key leaders plus anything that might help a reporter fill out a story, like fact sheets, industry trends, etc.

Be Crisis-Ready: Anticipate challenges and respond with transparency, speed, and empathy. Have a spokesperson plan.

Build Relationships That Matter: Foster genuine connections with journalists, influencers and audiences – ahead of when you might need their support.

> **Measure and Adapt**: Continuously refine your strategy based on data and evolving trends. Change is the constant. Expect it. Anticipate it. Plan for it.
>
> **Hire an Expert**: You don't have to go it alone. Some experts work with the media every day and know the challenges and secrets to getting coverage, outlets, and dos and don'ts. While publicists are often the first budget cut – they should be at the top of the budget spend list. When business is booming for all of your competitors, a good publicist will elevate you above the noise of the others. When business pulls back, a good publicist will keep you relevant, and front-and-center, making you and your company look stronger than you may be feeling.

In today's digital-first world, mastering media relations is more than merely managing the press -- it's about leading the narrative, building trust, and shaping your company's future. When CEOs lead with authenticity and clarity, they don't just navigate the media landscape -- they define it. In the next chapter, we'll dive into becoming an industry thought leader because this truly deserves a chapter of its own!

Chapter 27

Becoming an Industry Thought Leader:

The Empowering Influence of Authentic Storytelling

In today's fast-paced and highly connected world, being an industry thought leader is more than an accolade that can propel you into the Statusphere: It is a weighty responsibility and a powerful tool for influence. As a leader, you can shape conversations with all kinds of stakeholders, ignite innovation, and inspire trust. Thought leadership isn't about self-promotion: It is about making a significant meaningful contribution to the news landscape, while also helping others understand your industry including its challenges and solutions, as well as, maybe, its societal contributions.

Done correctly, authentic storytelling is at the heart of thought-leadership positioning. The leaders that get the free media coverage you want, earn their placements in print, broadcast and digital outlets. How is this? They've received coveted free media coverage because they have learned to tell stories that breathe life into their ideas, clearly communicate their vision, and understand the importance of connecting with each outlet's unique audience on a deeper level.

This chapter explores leveraging storytelling to your advantage so you can build credibility, inspire action and stand apart as a leader who actively shapes the future.

Why Thought Leadership Matters

It is worth your time, energy and budget considerations to do what is necessary to get yourself acknowledged and booked as an industry thought leader.

Thought-leadership positioning…

> **Builds Credibility and Trust:** Thoughtful storytelling positions you as a trusted voice in your industry. This can help define decision-making by partners, clients, employees, shareholders and stakeholders.
>
> **Earns Respect**: When your insights are in the media, you are getting a priceless "third-party endorsement" because the outlet chose you to help them tell a story. Whether it's a magazine, newspaper, website or TV/cable or radio show – someone believed you are the person who can help their news station or publication to garner more eyeballs and clicks than their competition – so they're giving you free airtime. The compilation of all these factors helps to inspire the confidence of customers, employees, investors and others.
>
> **Differentiates the Company**: Sharing your unique perspectives in media articles and interviews sets your company apart in a crowded marketplace.
>
> **Positions you as a Leader of Conversations**: When you innovate ideas, others follow your lead. The media allows you the opportunity to tell the world all about what you're doing – for free.

Strengthens Brand Reputation: A strong personal brand as a leader elevates not only your reputation, but the entire company's reputation as well.

Attracts Opportunities: Talent, partnerships and investors gravitate toward companies led by visionaries. The media-at-large wants visionary thought-leaders to make predictions, solve problems, explain industry relevance and also even comment on news issued by competitors within the sector.

Visibility Drives Business Growth: Increased recognition from earned media placements builds trust. In turn, this holds the potential to open doors to new markets and collaborations.

The Power of Storytelling in Thought Leadership

To become a thought leader who is valued by the media, you'll want to understand the hows and whys of storytelling. Remember, public relations (PR) earned media placements are not advertisements. Considering this, you want to make sure you are telling a story in a way that doesn't look, feel or seem like an advertisement for you or your company. If the editorial department of any outlet feels like you are using their editorial pages as a personal or corporate advertisement – your story will never make it to the print or airwaves. Or, if it does, it will be the only time you'll have been called upon to be an objective thought-leader.

To start getting the best media bookings, you will want to…

Humanize Your Message: Make whatever you want to say personal by bringing your personality to the interview along with relevant stories. Relatable narratives connect emotionally with audiences.

Be Real: Share your authentic self if you want to use your media moments to build loyalty and trust. (And, yes, you do want this!)

Simplify the Complex: The best thought leaders know how to break down complex stories without using industry jargon.

Connect the Dots: Storytelling is the tool you use to make technical concepts relatable and actionable. Learn to do this well and you will be in high demand for all kinds of broadcast and print content.

Evoke Emotion: Think about watching a compelling show on television or cable. What makes you keep watching is how you feel. Stories that stir curiosity, hope or ambition tend to compel audiences to act.

Guide The Journey: Every industry has challenges. Smart leaders find the opportunities within those challenges. Great thought leaders – coveted by the media for commentary – know how to show the way forward through their narrative. They may not have all the answers, but they have plenty of ideas for audiences to consider.

Demonstrate Authenticity: When it comes to news-worthy interviews, leaders who share what they know, but also share vulnerability about challenges, past or present, and lessons learned tend to inspire greater audience response. And, rest assured, the data trackers are assessing which thought leaders are helping the show get the best ratings.

Crafting Your Authentic Narrative

Being transparent during media interviews is a skill. While at times it can feel uncomfortable, with practice, you can learn and apply the skills you need to feel like a natural whether opining for print or broadcast outlets. Here are things to consider:

Define Your Perspective: Your personal experience and expertise matter. Focus your commentary on areas where your knowledge and experience shine.

Own Your Vision: Share your unique outlook on your industry's future. You are the expert who got the invite. Be you.

Provide Value: Offer actionable insights that solve problems or reveal opportunities.

Share Real Stories for Real Impact: Let the audience see the person behind the title. Your experiences are what make you relatable.

Celebrate Challenges: Highlight moments of adversity and the growth they inspired. No one's corporate career goes straight up. There are ups and downs and audiences like hearing about these rollercoaster rides.

Stay Consistent and Purposeful: Ensure your stories reflect your personal values and company mission. Remember to mention your company name when you can if it adds to the story. Every tale should reinforce what your company stands for.

Tailor Your Message: Know your audience! This is so important. Make sure the complexity of the story you share aligns with the readership or viewership of the outlet. For technical journals – be technical. For general news outlets – think about trends, problems, solutions, and opportunities on a broad scale. Customize your narrative for different stakeholders.

Speak Their Language: Skip the acronyms. To one person, M & A is marketing and advertising. To another it may mean mergers and acquisitions. Adapt your words and tone to resonate with the respective audience, without losing your authenticity.

Remember You are the Guest: This rule particularly applies to on-air broadcast interviews. The host invited you. You are the guest. Be polite. Respect that it is their show and you are the guest. Just like you wouldn't go to a party and eat the entire bowl of potato chips all by yourself – you don't appear on another's show and greedily try to steal all the airtime. If you do, don't expect an invite back from the outlet – or any others. Executive producers all watch competitor's programming. Rude guests don't get invites from anyone once their selfish nature is identified.

Keep your responses relevant, short and direct. Allow the host to hear what you have to say – and then lead you to the next question. They have their roles as hosts for a reason. They earned it by developing excellent on-air interviewing skills. Let them help you shine.

Steps to Becoming a Recognized Thought Leader

There are a variety of ways that you can get yourself positioned as an industry thought leader who is featured in plenty of free media coverage. Let's look at ways you can build your street cred.

Publish Valuable Content

- **Write Boldly**: Contact outlets and offer to contribute blogs, articles, and op-eds to share your perspective about topics trending or intriguing to the publication's audience. Don't worry about the size of the readership. Your first goal is to get published. Below, I'll share what you'll then do with that article!
- **Dive Deep**: Publish books or whitepapers if you have enough information to share because this will help to establish you as an authority, particularly when producers or editors are trying to pre-assess if you are the commentary expert they seek.

Speak on Prominent Platforms

- **Own the Stage**: Share your insights at conferences, webinars, and panels. Don't worry about receiving financial compensation. Everyone starts public speaking somewhere and it's usually without a check. That said, you are reaping rewards in other ways as you build your clout and reputation.
- **Lead Conversations**: Use every speaking opportunity to inspire and connect. Always consider a few key soundbites ahead of speaking to be sure you leave your audience with valuable and relevant information.

Leverage Digital Media

- **Be Social**: Use social platforms – any and all where you think you might find audience share. LinkedIn, X, Reddit, Quora and other platforms are free and offer you daily opportunities to engage with your existing audience and find new people as well.
- **Create Your Voice**: Podcasts and videos bring your leadership to life. These are great opportunities to keep your voice fresh and on point. The more you accept interviews, the better you'll get at delivering high-quality information in short soundbites.

Collaborate Strategically

- **Amplify with Allies**: Partner with influencers and others to broaden your reach.
- **Co-Create**: To enhance credibility, write, speak or host events with other thought leaders.

Build Your Community

- **Be Accessible**: Interact directly with your audience through Q&As and networking events.
- **Foster Connection**: Make engagement meaningful by valuing input and feedback.

Best Practices for Storytelling

There are a variety of best practices you will want to keep top-of-mind if you want to be a storytelling thought leader (and, let me assure you, you do!) Consider each of these carefully and figure out how you can implement the suggestions into your storytelling.

Be Transparent: Embrace honesty and, whenever possible, share your successes and failures with humility.

Show Growth: Highlight the lessons you've learned during those ups and downs to demonstrate your resilience and humanity.

Keep It Relatable: Speak simply using clear, relatable language. Try to draw on shared experiences and universal themes like perseverance or innovation to create a connection with audiences.

Balance Emotion with Logic: Let data merge with humanity. Use numbers to reinforce stories and stories to humanize data. At the same time, anchor the audiences' perceptions by inspiring with feeling but guiding expectations with reason.

Always End Interviews with Action: Invite engagement by concluding your stories with a call to action that sparks momentum. You can be subtle – or not! You do want them to buy your products or services…and your stock if you are publicly traded. So, remember to empower their decisions and leave your audience inspired to take the next step.

Case Study: Real-Life Inspiration through ReNuclear Now's Storytelling Success

THE CHALLENGE: ReNuclear Now's CEO sought to position the company as a leader in the nuclear and renewable energy space while elevating his personal profile as an industry authority.

THE SOLUTIONS:

Content Creation: A book about the energy landscape was published relatively quickly and for a reasonable price by compiling a series of previously written blogs and articles. The focus was to demystify nuclear energy and to showcase it as a cleaner energy alternative. Intrigue and greater interest were developed by blending personal stories with actionable, informative sustainable energy insights.

Speaking Engagements: Management leaders are committed to accepting any and all opportunities to share the company's mission. This included a mix of financial presentations, panels and establishing a consistent presence at major alternative energy conferences.

Digital Leadership: ReNuclear Now did a major website update – and it wasn't expensive as they used WordPress, which is an easy-to-navigate and update platform. The primary purpose of the website was to become "The Ultimate Repository of All Things Nuclear Energy-Related." Daily as content was being added, the company began engaging more with potentially relevant audiences by using LinkedIn and X to share tips, trends, ideas and both industry and corporate developments relating to nuclear energy. This included sharing ReNuclear Now's news developments; links to existing content on their website; general industry news; and, even sometimes the news developments of their competitors. Occasionally – when sharing competitor developments, the commentary was added. This helped media booking agents recognize that the ReNuclear Now team could opine and offer intelligent commentary about more than their own company -- but about the energy industry in general.

THE RESULTS: ReNuclear Now's recognition surged with increased customer loyalty and stronger partnerships. The CEO becoming a sought-after industry voice. Why? All of this ultimately created a significant amount of traffic to their website which became a library for public consumption – by all kinds of people – including new investors, industry analysts and the media.

Key Takeaways for Leaders in the Media Spotlight

> **Storytelling is Leadership**: Your authentic, unique narrative is your most powerful tool for connection. Don't be generic.
>
> **Inspire with Value and Never Over-Hype**: Every story should provide actionable insights and inspiration. Share your value proposition but keep it factual. Be aware

that you don't want to inadvertently appear to be giving guidance – or you'll be creating a regulatory nightmare and unnecessary investor pressure.

Consistency Wins: Align your story with your values and deliver it consistently across platforms. Remember in a digitally driven internet world – every one of your stakeholders will ultimately find your interview and assess how they perceive it applies to them and their relationship with you.

Be Relatable: Share your triumphs and challenges -- the human side of leadership inspires trust.

By embracing storytelling as a cornerstone of thought leadership, leaders don't just influence industry conversations -- they shape them. Your authentic voice is the spark that builds trust, drives action, and inspires change. Use it wisely.

Chapter 28

Communicating During a Crisis:

How Perceptive Leaders Go Forward with Clarity and Confidence

Communication isn't just about information in a crisis -- it's about leadership. Perceptive leadership, the ability to understand, anticipate and respond to stakeholders' emotions and concerns, distinguishes exceptional CEOs in challenging moments. Being a perceptive leader means reading between the lines, adapting your approach in real time, and ensuring that every action and word resonates authentically.

Crises test organizations and leadership's mettle. How a CEO communicates during uncertainty can inspire confidence, preserve trust, and even strengthen relationships.

This chapter is written to better equip you by highlighting many of the tools that are required to lead through a crisis, perceptively. For starters, this skillset will include combining empathy, strategic insight, and clear messaging to navigate whatever challenges arise.

Why Crisis Communication Requires Perceptive Leadership

Let's review perception again. Perceptions are the result of thoughts merging with feelings. All day long, consciously or not, our minds are processing all kinds of stimuli in an attempt to interpret our worlds and those who live within them. During stressful times, the feelings that result from "I'm frightened" thoughts can become super-glued in our memory banks – again, possibly without any conscious awareness that this is happening. Nonetheless, it is this merger of thoughts and feelings that forms our beliefs that underlies the perceptions -- or the unique operating systems -- through which each of us sees ourselves, others, and everything else we encounter.

In light of this, understanding the impact of perceptions and being a perceptive leader is of paramount importance. Let's explore perception a bit and look at why it is so important for leaders to consider.

A perceptive leader…

- Considers, assesses and addresses areas for different perspectives from all counterparties before negotiations, announcements, interactions and overall communication points.
- Monitors and adjusts communication based on how the message is received, not just how it's delivered.
- Builds credibility and attentiveness by fostering trust, particularly when possibly having to acknowledge potential known and unknown factors.
- Tries consistently to anticipate potential areas of confusion or fear. This enables them to address concerns before they escalate, instilling a sense of control and preparedness.

- **Stays** attuned to emerging issues to ensure swift and effective action, making shareholders and stakeholders feel that the leader is agile and adaptive in their crisis response.
- In times of crisis, recognize the crucial importance of employee morale and do their best to connect with their employees on an emotional level. Perceptive leaders know that acknowledging employee fears and concerns, while providing reassurance in whatever ways possible, can go a long way in maintaining morale and trust.
- Also acknowledges employee emotions and their need to feel heard and valued, especially during times of uncertainty. Yes, sometimes you'll want to scream – "but we're all adults" yet, trust that taking this extra step, can make a big difference in outcomes.
- Understands that customers, investors and partners may each have different priorities so messaging is considered and possibly adjusted accordingly.
- Knows they are reinforcing their leadership prowess—when stakeholders see a CEO responding insightfully and decisively it strengthens long-term confidence.

Building a Crisis Communication Plan with Perception in Mind

Nobody likes a crisis – but it can still be an opportunity to shine and instill confidence. So, how can you build a crisis management plan that considers all the thoughts, feelings and emotions that are likely to arise from various stakeholders and shareholders – each with different agendas?

Here are a few key considerations to percolate.

Anticipate Scenarios with Stakeholders in Focus

- **Assess Risks Perceptively**: Go beyond operational challenges to identify the emotional and reputational risks of potential crises.

- **Scenario Mapping**: Consider how different audiences might react to each scenario and plan communications accordingly.

Assemble a Perceptive Crisis Team

- **Empower Emotional Intelligence**: Include leaders who excel at understanding and responding to diverse stakeholder needs. Hire an established perception analyst with crisis management experience. I know one if you don't. ;-)
- **Clarify Roles**: Ensure each team member knows who is responsible for delivering information and addressing concerns.

Create Adaptive Messaging Frameworks

- **Define Core Statements with Flexibility**: Prepare adaptable messages that can shift in tone or detail as the crisis unfolds.
- **Write Audience-Centric Communication**: Tailor drafts for internal teams, customers, media, and investors, acknowledging their unique perspectives. Merge messages accordingly with eyes wide open that messages to one group might still be seen by others…especially if that information or opinion makes it onto some social media page.

Monitor and Respond in Real-Time

- **Stay Perceptively Attuned**: Use social listening tools and define direct feedback channels to gauge sentiment and adjust communication, if situations change or sentiment temperatures start to rise.
- **Be Agile**: Recognize when a message needs reframing or further clarity based on how it is being received. This is never ideal – but it happens. So, don't let egos prevent you and/or others on your team from providing updates – and even outright corrections, if necessary – especially as additional information is revealed.

Practice Empathy in Preparedness

- **Crisis Simulations**: Train your team to consider not just the operational response but the emotional responses of various classifications of stakeholders.
- **Debrief for Growth**: After drills, reflect on the overall perceptiveness of the team's communications and also the subsequent responses to the messaging to improve future responses.

Dos and Don'ts of Perceptive Crisis Communication

Let's look at both dos and don'ts that you'll want to consider for yourself, and when leading your team.

Be Transparent with Understanding: Acknowledge the crisis early and show you are aware of the concerns of your shareholder and stakeholder audiences. Share what you know while openly communicating the next steps.

Act Quickly with Awareness: Issue an initial statement promptly, demonstrating you're both responsive and in control. Use updates to modify messaging as additional information becomes available and/or disclosable, and, adapt accordingly to the shifting sentiments of stakeholders, if necessary.

Empathize Fully: Recognize the impact of the crisis on all stakeholders, from employees to customers. Use language that reflects genuine care and actionable support.

Stay Consistent Across Channels: Align messaging to ensure trust and clarity, avoiding contradictions or mixed signals. Know that anyone disgruntled – and there will be someone disgruntled – will figure out how to make the world see whatever you are saying or doing. Continually reinforce a central narrative while adapting it for different audiences.

Focus on Solutions with Vision: Be the leader and take the lead. Highlight the steps being taken to address the crisis and reassure stakeholders of your company's resilience.

Avoid Guesswork: Remember this: "The news is rarely as good or as bad as the first report." In light of this, speak only to what you know for certain because speculation erodes credibility and retractions are even worse.

Don't Be Defensive: Maybe you are directly responsible for the problem, maybe you are not. Either way, as the leader of an organization – the responsibility to manage the situation falls on your shoulders, as are the expectations that you will lead and find a resolution or define the path forward. Accept accountability where appropriate and focus on problem-solving, not blame-shifting.

Don't Overwhelm with Details: Keep all of your messaging clear and concise. Avoid unnecessary complexity. It will only get misinterpreted and it holds the potential to elevate anger.

Don't Ignore Employee Needs: Keep internal audiences informed to prevent rumors and sustain morale.

Avoid Being Silent: Not having all the answers when it is time to make a statement can be very uncomfortable. But you cannot shirk your responsibility of making a statement. You can say: "We are gathering information in real-time." No one is going to love that answer – but at least they'll know someone is in charge and trying to fill in the answer blanks. Ignore this at your peril. Be assured that your lack of communication will 100% invite unfavorable speculation and will damage trust.

Case Study: SecureSure Data's Perceptive Leadership

THE SITUATION: SecureSure Data, a cybersecurity leader, was targeted by ransomware that disrupted operations and exposed customer data.

THE ACTIONS:

Immediate Transparency: The CEO acknowledged the breach promptly, empathizing with customer concerns and outlining immediate actions.

Customer Reassurance: Dedicated support channels provided timely and consistent updates. A hotline service was temporarily added to speak with clients.

Insightful Media Engagement: A press conference call clearly addressed the crisis, demonstrating accountability and forward-thinking prevention plans.

Proactive Solutions: SecureSure Data announced enhancements to its cybersecurity systems. Throughout the following months, the Company continued to provide updates and assurances that the situation had been remedied and additional preventive strategies were in place. Every message emphasized a long-term commitment to each stakeholder vertical.

THE RESULTS: Nobody was happy with the data breach. However, the Company was able to minimize customer churn and ultimately restored trust. By being very transparent about actions that were being taken to prevent such an event from occurring again, the leadership team managed to reinforce its reputation as a responsible industry partner.

CEO Takeaways for Perceptive Crisis Communication

While nobody looks forward to a crisis, they happen and smart leaders prepare by considering a variety of scenarios, assessing weaknesses, addressing potential threats and coming up with a "fill in the blanks" plan in the event one is necessary.

Key perceptive takeaways to keep in mind include the following:

> **Do Your Best to Lead with Empathy**: Take the time to authentically understand and address the various stakeholders' concerns – doing so as thoroughly and carefully as possible.
>
> **Stay Ahead of Sentiment**: Monitor and adjust communication to reflect audience reactions.
>
> **Align Strategy with Emotion**: Balance operational updates with emotional intelligence to build trust.
>
> **Consistency is Key**: Ensure all messaging reinforces the same core narrative while tailoring it for each audience.
>
> **Turn Crisis into Opportunity**: Use the challenge to demonstrate the strength of your leadership and your organization's resilience.

Perceptive leadership during a crisis isn't just about managing the situation -- it's about understanding the hearts and minds of those affected. As hard as it may be to imagine in those moments of crisis, leadership teams can transform challenges into defining moments of trust, resilience, and growth by leading with empathy, insight, and strategic clarity.

Chapter 29

Keeping Employees Motivated and Aligned During Times of Change:

Perceptive Leadership and Mastering Internal Messaging

Change is an inevitable part of business, driven by various factors such as market dynamics, technological innovations, mergers, and/or economic pressures. However, for employees, change often brings about feelings of uncertainty, anxiety and resistance. This is where the role of perceptive leadership, particularly that of the CEO, becomes crucial. A leader who is attuned to their employees' emotions, concerns and aspirations can transform moments of change into opportunities for alignment and growth.

In the digital age, the significance of internal messaging cannot be overstated. Every word -- whether spoken in a town hall or written in an email -- carries weighty risk, as it can be shared by any recipient publicly and anonymously.

This chapter is designed to empower leaders to craft clear, empathetic and perceptive communications. These types of messages have the power to keep employees motivated, aligned, and focused, while also safeguarding the company's culture and reputation.

The Role of Perceptive Leadership in Internal Messaging

Perceptive leaders are always focused on maintaining open lines of communication with all levels of employees. Having a strategy in place before you might need one -- due to any number of necessary corporate pivots make one necessary -- is smart leadership and corporate success planning. Here are a variety of reasons why you always want to stay ahead on the internal communications curve.

Solid Internal Communications Strategies….

Build Trust: By "employing" an attuned listener strategy, you will build trust and be far better able to understand employees' concerns.

Reassure Through Clarity: Clear internal communication plans reduce uncertainty, reinforce confidence in leadership and cut down on the coffee klatch chatter and cocktail hour assumptions.

Align Vision and Goals: Done correctly and consistently, internal communications pave the way to framing changes within the larger narrative of the company's mission and vision.

Create Role Awareness: Help your employees see their unique contributions to your organizational objectives. Every role – from the receptionist to you at the helm – is essential for success. Reinforce this belief with your teams by reminding them regularly of their importance to the entirety of the organization.

Maintain Productivity: By addressing questions and concerns before they escalate into distractions, lots of problems can be resolved.

Foster Focus: By providing the tools and clarity that employees need to remain engaged you're already ahead of any number of issues.

Reinforce Culture: Messaging can be used to emphasize the organization's core values, before, during and after any transitions.

Build Unity: Good messaging that is consistent strengthens a shared sense of purpose and belonging.

Challenges of Internal Messaging in a Hyper-Connected Era

Internal messaging has never been more challenging than it is today. Leaders want to keep their employees informed – yet every single statement runs the very real risk of being publicly disseminated. As such, the temptation is to say nothing: Not a great communications strategy for a company that wants to grow.

Let's acknowledge the risks and then review principles for best practices in internal messaging.

THE RISKS:

Instant Digital Exposure: Internal messages can become public, sometimes distorting the intended message.

Authenticity Can Be Guarded: Desiring to ensure messaging reflects well on the company, even if exposed externally, can make even the best of intended messaging feel inauthentic.

Navigating Misinformation: Messaging can trigger speculation that you'd ideally like to prevent. Lack of clarity can lead to rumors and distrust.

Not Countering Quickly Enough: Lack of real-time updates to address inaccuracies is a challenge for even the best communicators.

Inconsistency and Lack of Unified Messaging: Misalignment between departments creates confusion and undermines leadership credibility.

Principles of Effective Internal Messaging

To effectively lead internal messaging, the following should always be considered.

- **Regularly remind employees that "Loose lips sink ships."** Encourage regular reminders by all leaders to their teams of the benefits of enthusiastically maintaining internal confidentiality. Such confidentiality is not only for the health of the Company – but, accordingly, for the jobs of the employees, as well.
- **Acknowledge Uncertainty**: Be honest about unknowns while providing a clear context for decisions.
- **Share the Why**: Explain the rationale behind any necessary changes, tying the decision(s) to long-term goals for a healthy, viable company.
- **Personalize Messages**: Address how changes may impact employees both professionally and personally. Be sincere and forthright.
- **Support Through Action**: Highlight tangible resources like training or counseling.
- **Unify Leadership Messaging**: Ensure every leader communicates aligned narratives. Do not tolerate exceptions.
- **Establish Cadence**: Communicate regularly to maintain trust even when updates are minimal.
- **Show a Path Forward**: Emphasize how challenges are being addressed.
- **Empower and Encourage Contribution**: Provide actionable steps for employees to feel engaged and involved.

Best Practices for Perceptive Internal Messaging

There are a variety of best practices that are worthy of practical implementation. Here goes!

Use Diverse Communication Channels
- **Town Halls**: Create open forums for direct interaction.
- **Emails and Memos**: Provide structured, detailed updates.
- **Digital Platforms**: Use intranets or tools like Slack to ensure real-time communication.

Tailor Messages for Specific Audiences
- **Frontline Employees**: Focus on immediate impacts and practical steps.
- **Managers**: Equip them with resources to guide their teams effectively.
- **Executives**: Provide high-level updates with strategic metrics.

Monitor Sentiment Continuously
- **Surveys**: Use polls to track morale and identify communication gaps.
- **Listening Sessions**: Provide safe spaces for employees to voice concerns.
- **Anonymous Feedback**: Create mechanisms for candid input to uncover unseen issues.

Prepare for Potential Leaks
- **Message with Integrity**: Assume all internal communication could become public and craft messages accordingly.
- **Crisis Contingencies**: Have a plan for responding to leaked or misinterpreted information.

CEO Takeaways for Perceptive Leadership During Changing Times

You have a unique opportunity to lead through change by harnessing the power of perceptive insights and mastering internal messaging in a world that demands connection and trust. With clear, empathetic communication as your leadership superpower, you can inspire alignment, motivation, and most importantly, high levels of employee engagement. This is a key factor in setting the foundation for a thriving organization, and it underscores the crucial role that CEOs play in motivating their teams.

In the event of a crisis, as CEO you'll want to engage with your employees by…

- **Communicating Early**: Get ahead of rumors with timely updates.
- **Being Accessible**: Hold space for one-on-one or small-group conversations.
- **Using Positive Framing**: Highlight opportunities and shared progress.
- **Encouraging Feedback**: Listen actively and adapt as needed.
- **Avoiding Silence**: Gaps in communication fuel anxiety.
- **Not Downplaying Concerns**: Acknowledge challenges honestly.
- **Avoiding Jargon**: Speak clearly and directly to ensure understanding.
- **Not Overpromising**: Be realistic about what can be achieved and when.

Next, let's move onto the personal and private side of leadership.

Section VII

The Private and Personal Side of Leadership

Chapter 30

The Loneliness of Leadership:

Strategies for Maintaining Perspective and Connection

Leadership at the top can be paradoxical -- undeniably rewarding but often profoundly isolating. As CEOs shoulder the ultimate responsibility for their organizations, the weight of decisions, scrutiny, and expectations can lead to an unspoken loneliness that undermines even the most capable executives. The key to thriving in the CEO environment lies in perceptive leadership: staying attuned to oneself, others, and the broader mission.

This chapter offers actionable strategies to help leaders address isolation, maintain meaningful connections, and lead with emotional resilience and clarity. Perceptive leaders recognize that loneliness is not a weakness but a self-challenge that can be transformed into an opportunity for growth and deeper engagement with oneself and others.

Why Leadership Can Feel Lonely

There are a variety of very real reasons why being a leader can be a lonely place. Let's look at them.

- **The Weight of Accountability**: Ultimately all the good developments, yet particularly the bad, are perceived as 100% the responsibility of the CEO regardless of how many management layers a company has. Also, the reality is that a CEO might have to make any number of decisions that could potentially affect the livelihood of hundreds of employees. This level of responsibility can be overwhelming and isolating.
- **Solitary Decisions**: High-stakes choices often rest solely on the CEO, reinforcing a sense of isolation. If the choice ultimately is well received optically by shareholders and stakeholders – the CEO is a winner. If not, the decision may set the stage for an unpleasant and highly public ouster.
- **Confidentiality Barriers**: Sharing concerns internally can feel risky. Sharing them externally may make a CEO question whether their confidant of choice truly understands the challenge or decision they are contemplating – and also if they are trustworthy.
- **Navigating Authority**: Balancing transparency with a leadership presence can unintentionally create distance. Many are afraid to do anything to bridge those distances because they wonder how boundaries will then be pushed or exploited.
- **Constant Scrutiny**: Burdens of perception are real: Employees, shareholders, stakeholders and the media are a constant: People will always be examining each and every action and statement of key leaders.
- **Pressure to Perform**: The need to project confidence seemingly at all times, and particularly when the most difficult decisions must be made, can prevent leaders from seeking the support they need, when needed.
- **Disconnect from Day-to-Day Realities**: Depending upon the size of the company -- or even just a leader's style of engaging -- CEOs can feel removed

from employees' frontline experiences. This can create a very real divide, or a perceived one.
- **Challenges in Relatability**: Maintaining an overview of the big picture sometimes means losing sight of individual experiences. While there are similarities in any leadership role, every CEO's role in different. Finding those with whom you feel you can relate, trust and rely upon is a challenge.

The Risks of Leadership Isolation

Leaders who ignore their feelings of isolation are making a serious leadership mistake for a few very identifiable reasons.

- Decision-making can become narrow without diverse perspectives. This can lead to echo chambers or blind spots that may result in impaired decision-making.
- The relentless pressures of leadership, unmitigated by emotional support, can lead to stress, disengagement, and diminished energy. Emotional burnout at the top is real.
- A lack of meaningful connections with employees and stakeholders can erode a leader's ability to understand and address their needs. The potential lack of empathy can affect a leader's relatability and dampen employee motivation.
- Distance between CEOs and their teams can foster perceptions of disconnect, reducing morale and loyalty. This can hurt everyone's sense of trust.

Strategies for Overcoming Leadership Loneliness

Do you have to be lonely now that you're at an enviable pinnacle? No. Absolutely not! There are a lot of things you can do to counter the feelings of leadership isolation.

Build a Trusted Inner Circle

- Join CEO forums or advisory groups to exchange ideas and share experiences in a confidential environment. Peer networks can be priceless.

- Hire a professional you trust. Interview and find someone with whom you can confide without worry, to gain perspective, enhance decision-making, and develop leadership strategies.
- Foster open, constructive dialogue with trusted colleagues or board members who can offer support and insights. Share challenges to develop genuine connections, request advice and listen. Ultimately the decisions are yours, but sometimes just hearing yourself speak aloud about an issue, getting asked pertinent questions or listening to how someone might handle a situation, can reinforce or even shift your ideas constructively.
- **Empower Others**: Delegate authority to senior executives to create a collaborative leadership environment. Ask others how they would solve a problem if it was their responsibility.
- **Stay Connected to Employees**: Hold one-on-one conversations, town halls, or informal check-ins to bridge the gap with employees.
- **Walk the Floor**: Spend time in the workplace to gain firsthand insights into team dynamics and challenges. This will help you see and hear what might otherwise go unobserved and unheard – plus your employees will appreciate your presence.
- **Feedback Channels**: Create open pathways for employees to share ideas and perspectives directly with leadership. Provide an anonymous suggestion box. Actually read the suggestions.
- **Invest in Personal Well-Being**: Learn and use meditation, hypnosis or reflection journaling to stay centered and manage stress.
- **Physical Health**: Prioritize exercise, sleep and nutrition to build resilience and sustain energy. Remember: If you think you don't have the time, imagine what could happen if you actually got sick and must be out for an extended period.
- **Personal Passions**: Dedicate time to activities outside of work that rejuvenate and inspire you. As the saying goes: All work and no play make Jack a dull boy. Balance is important and your interests make you interesting.
- **Mentorship**: Seek out and cultivate relationships with other seasoned leaders to gain perspective and learn from their experiences. You're never too old to find a mentor.

- **Industry Networks**: Engage with peers through associations or events to broaden your circle of support.
- **Community Involvement**: Participate in charitable or local initiatives to stay grounded and connected to a broader purpose.

The Role of Perspective in Leadership

Maintaining perspective is always an important life skill. For leaders, particularly CEOs, it is all the more important. How can you do it? Here are a variety of considerations to contemplate.

> **Focus on the Bigger Picture**: Regularly revisit the mission, vision and goals you outlined for your company when you accepted the responsibilities of leadership. This will help you to stay inspired and aligned – and maybe inspire tweaks. Likewise, reflect on your personal values to maintain a clear sense of purpose and direction. Find ways to bridge any gaps you observe.
>
> **Embrace Continuous Learning:** Seek out diverse perspectives through books, conferences, or conversations with thought leaders. Keep broadening your awareness. This will help you to view challenges as opportunities for growth, as you also refine your approach with each experience. Biographies of accomplished people – who've reached the pinnacles in any arena -- can provide all kinds of insight, personal validation and comfort, too.
>
> **Balance Confidence with Humility:** Recognizing that no leader has all the answers is essential. If you accept that you're not alone – when you may feel as if you are – you will be far more open to actively seeking input from others. This is a massive step in the right direction for reducing a sense of loneliness and upping your leadership game and network. Also, when seeking to balance confidence and humility, remember: We all do a lot alone, but we also can't do plenty without the commitment and contributions of our co-workers. Celebrate the contributions of your team to foster collaboration and shared purpose. While you might not be

"all-in" equally, you are all part of the ultimate success you envision as a leader. The more you showcase that attitude sincerely, the more you'll build an enthusiastic team of supporters.

Key Takeaways for CEOs

Loneliness is Normal: It's important to acknowledge the isolating nature of leadership and take proactive steps to address it. Remember, you're not alone in this struggle.

Connection is the Key: Building meaningful relationships within and outside the organization can help you find support from people you can trust. Remember, your connections are not just a part of your life, they are a crucial part of your leadership path and growth.

Perspective Sustains Purpose: Staying grounded in your mission and values is not just a task, it's a necessity. It helps maintain focus and resilience, and reminds you why you're in this position in the first place.

Strength Through Vulnerability: Sharing challenges authentically enhances trust and inspires loyalty among employees and stakeholders.

Reflect Regularly: Dedicate time for self-reflection via mindfulness practices.

Avoid Isolation: Resist the urge to withdraw during challenging times.

Don't Ignore Feedback: Embrace constructive criticism as an opportunity for growth. What you may be getting is critical information.

Beware of Overextending Yourself: Delegate effectively to prevent burnout and foster team collaboration. If you get sick, there will be even bigger problems.

By addressing the loneliness of leadership with perceptive strategies, CEOs can cultivate meaningful connections, sustain their well-being, and lead with greater clarity and confidence.

Connection is not just a remedy for isolation -- it is the foundation of transformative leadership.

Chapter 31

Maintaining Energy, Building Resilience, and Avoiding Burnout:

The Perceptive Leader's Guide to Sustainable Success

The role of a CEO demands boundless energy, sharp focus, and unshakable resilience. However, the threat of burnout looms even for the most driven leaders. In today's high-pressure environments, perceptive leaders recognize that the key to avoiding burnout isn't about enduring a storm, but about proactively managing energy, fostering emotional agility, and laying the groundwork for sustainable leadership. This strategic approach to resilience is crucial in today's business landscape.

As we explored in the last chapter, burnout is a very real and significant issue. In this chapter, we're going to delve deeper into this crucial topic, providing you with more actionable insights to help you sustain peak performance, protect your well-being, and lead with strength, clarity, and purpose over the long term.

Perceptive leadership is not just about preventing burnout, it's about inspiring teams to adopt balanced and resilient approaches. As a CEO, your role is not just pivotal, it's integral to the success of your team's well-being and performance.

The Causes of Burnout

Burnout, a universal experience that can happen to anyone at any stage of life, is particularly significant for leaders. The constant demands of decision-making, problem-solving, and accountability can lead to mental and emotional exhaustion. Isolation, as we discussed in the last chapter, exacerbates feelings of pressure and self-doubt. Add overextending yourself and neglecting personal needs while juggling competing priorities, and you have the perfect recipe for energy and focus to be drained in real time.

The Impact of Burnout

Burnout impacts the ability to lead in several ways. For starters, lack of sleep -- from stress, long hours, or lack of exercise -- leads to extended fatigue, which can easily cloud judgment, stifle creativity, and/or diminish the ability to think strategically. This hurts decision-making ability. Both professional and personal strain can manifest in any number of ways, which can create an erosion of trust and connection.

Prolonged stress elevates the risk of physical and mental health challenges, from heart disease to depression. It's crucial to recognize the signs of burnout, even if you might not think you're under stress (or want to admit it). These signs may be becoming apparent. This can include persistent fatigue, sleep issues, or frequent illnesses; increased irritability, anxiety, or detachment; procrastination, reduced productivity, or withdrawal from interaction. Being informed and proactive about recognizing these signs can help you take control of your well-being and prevent burnout.

So, if any of this sounds familiar, or if you just want to make sure you avoid elevating your burnout risk, here are a variety of things you'll want to seriously consider.

To maintain energy, you'll need to prioritize physical health, manage mental energy and replenish emotional energy. You can do this by…

- Incorporating activities that boost endurance, strength, and flexibility to enhance energy.
- Embrace a diet rich in whole foods to fuel optimal brain and body function.
- Establish a calming bedtime routine and commit to 7–8 hours of restorative sleep each night. If you can't get adequate sleep every night – do whatever it takes to make sure you're getting it at least every other night – and…
- Manage energy by learning and practicing meditation, hypnosis and breathing exercises to control thoughts and reduce stress.
- Stretch often. Sitting all day? Get up and stretch for a solid 1-3 minutes every hour.
- Eliminate multitasking to improve efficiency and engagement. Focus on one task at a time.
- Step away at intervals to recharge and maintain cognitive sharpness. Take a mid-day walk.
- Celebrate wins. Recognize both personal and team achievements to sustain motivation. Reflect on positive moments to counterbalance challenges.
- Spend time with mentors, friends, or loved ones who rejuvenate your spirit.
- Establish clear limits to your workday to protect personal time. Yes, you're busy, but you can enjoy an uninterrupted dinner.
- Delegate and empower your team to handle tasks – including those in high-impact areas.
- Learn to say "No." Protect your bandwidth by declining commitments that don't align with strategic priorities.
- Manage large objectives by dividing them into achievable steps. Break down big projects into a series of do-able milestones.
- Vacations and weekend downtime are essential.
- Hobbies are important. Cultivate interests outside of work to maintain perspective and joy.

- Read.
- Plan relaxing with family and friends

Key Takeaways for Perceptive Leaders

Energy is a Resource: Treat your physical, mental, and emotional energy as invaluable and prioritize replenishment.

Resilience is Learnable: With the right tools and mindset, you can cultivate resilience through practicing mindfulness skills, being adaptable, and creating strong support systems.

Burnout is Preventable. You can prevent burnout by setting proactive boundaries, scheduling recovery, and maintaining a sustainable pace.

Leadership is Holistic. Effective leaders model balanced, resilient behaviors that inspire their teams to do the same. This sets the stage for getting the job(s) done even more efficiently.

You Have the Time. If you don't think you have the time now to prioritize your mental and physical well-being, imagine being forced to prioritize it because you've gotten ill or incapacitated in some way.

Sustainable leadership starts with self-awareness. By prioritizing energy management and building resilience, perceptive CEOs ensure they can lead effectively and sustainably, which results in increased productivity, better team morale, and reduced turnover. As a leader, when you take care of yourself, you are giving a "Show not Tell" to your employees. Ultimately, demonstrating self-care empowers your teams to follow suit, creating a culture of success and well-being.

Chapter 32

The Power of Continuous Learning:

Staying Curious and Adaptive in a Fast-Changing World

For CEOs, the ability to learn, adapt, and evolve is no longer a luxury -- it is an essential hallmark of exceptional leadership. In a world of accelerating technological advancements, market shifts, and continually shifting customer expectations -- staying curious and committed to lifelong learning is the key to navigating complexity and driving success. Leaders who embrace continuous learning inspire adaptability, innovation, and resilience across their organizations, setting a standard capable of fueling growth at every level.

This chapter illuminates the strategic importance of continuous learning while providing actionable approaches to encourage your curiosity and adaptability. It guides you on how to lead your organization through this mindset, empowering you to achieve sustainable success.

The Critical Role of Continuous Learning for CEOs:

Being a lifelong learner is not just a necessity, it's a strategic advantage. Continuous learning equips CEOs with the insights and flexibility to pivot plans and strategies effectively in response to new challenges: It can make all the difference in establishing and maintaining a competitive edge while growing a business that can navigate uncertain business climates while also finding new ways to drive innovation ahead of the competition.

Key considerations as to why continual learning is paramount for leaders include any of the following:

- The rapid evolution of technology, markets, and regulations requires leaders who can confidently anticipate and adapt.
- By committing to learning, CEOs gain the insights and flexibility to pivot strategies effectively in response to new challenges -- empowering them to confidently steer their organizations through uncertainty.
- Staying informed exposes leaders to diverse perspectives, groundbreaking ideas, and cutting-edge technologies that fuel transformative solutions.
- A curious mindset fosters creativity, encouraging exploration of unconventional approaches to solve complex problems.
- Lifelong learning empowers CEOs to view setbacks as stepping stones, turning obstacles into opportunities for growth.
- Adaptability allows leaders to stay composed during disruptions while ensuring their organizations remain focused and agile.
- CEOs who model a growth mindset inspire employees to embrace change and pursue their professional development. Establishing a culture of continuous learning for all drives higher employee engagement, retention and performance -- laying the foundation for greater organizational success.

Practical Strategies for Staying Curious and Adaptive:

As it's important to cultivate a growth mindset, stay informed and engage in active learning -- let's review a strategic roadmap that you can use to create a learning culture in your organization, and lead by example.

- **See Leadership as a Journey**: Embrace Leadership as a process of continuous growth.
- **Welcome Challenges**: Treat every new situation as a chance to expand your skills and understanding. In the aftermath, when you debrief, continue to frame the situation as a past challenge that's now been overcome.
- **Seek Honest Feedback**: Regularly engage peers, mentors and employees to uncover areas for improvement while determining pathways to practically bring those improvements to realities.
- **Engage with Industry Trends**: Read extensively, including industry news, books and white papers.
- **Follow Visionaries**: Learn from thought leaders to gain fresh perspectives. There are new books every year to read along with plenty of classics. Then, there are podcasts to tune into and social feeds on Linkedin and elsewhere where you can find plenty of ideas for leaders you admire.
- **Leverage Digital Learning**: Consider webinars and online courses to stay on the cutting edge. Many colleges offer free classes that you can audit.
- **Experiment and Iterate**: Test innovative ideas in low-risk environments and learn by doing.
- **Attend Networking Events**: Seek opportunities to mix, mingle and exchange insights with peers at conferences, workshops and other professional gatherings.
- **Collaborate with Mentors**: Learn from experienced leaders who can provide invaluable guidance.
- **Build Inclusive Teams**: Surround yourself with individuals from varied backgrounds and expertise.
- **Encourage Constructive Open Dialogue**: Promote a workplace where everyone feels empowered to share ideas without fear. That said, frame the

sharing as "While you might point out a problem, please couple that with a solution."
- **Collaborate Across Boundaries**: Partner with leaders, if possible, in other industries for fresh approaches and solutions.

Critical Takeaways for Visionary CEOs

Remember…

Curiosity Powers Leadership: Staying curious is fundamental to navigating complexity and inspiring others.

Learning Fuels Innovation: Continuous learning unlocks possibilities and fosters creativity.

Adaptability Drives Resilience: Embracing change better equips leaders to tackle challenges with greater confidence.

Lead the Learning Movement: Demonstrate a growth mindset and champion a culture of learning.

By prioritizing continuous learning, CEOs position themselves and their organizations for enduring success. In a world that evolves faster every day, the leaders who thrive are those who embrace curiosity and adaptability as cornerstones of their leadership philosophy.

Chapter 33

Building Your Legacy:

Ensuring Your Impact Endures

As a CEO, your tenure may be finite, but your impact has the potential to last indefinitely. Building a legacy isn't just about achieving business milestones or delivering short-term results: It's about shaping a resilient organization, empowering its people, and embedding a purpose that will thrive long after your departure. A well-crafted legacy reflects your achievements and the transformative influence you've had on the organization's culture, vision and long-term success.

This chapter provides actionable strategies for consciously building a legacy that institutionalizes your values, develops future leaders, and ensures a culture of excellence that defines your organization for years to come.

The Importance of Legacy-Building

You want to build a strong legacy because it is the foundation that ensures your organization will continue to grow and flourish, sustaining its momentum even after you've stepped away. Every day, everything you do has the potential to establish your company as a stand-alone, formidable industry player, a partner to other companies, or an acquisition candidate by a larger conglomerate. Whatever the end-game, you'll always want to make sure that your shares become an annuity for your work, meaning that the value of your shares will continue to generate income or benefits for you and your stakeholders and that your shareholders cheer your accomplishments because you, your vision, and your efforts also helped others win.

By building a legacy correctly, you'll leave behind a series of robust systems and cultural norms you've established, which will help the organization weather future leadership transitions and external challenges with resilience. Leaving a legacy gives your leadership purpose and affirms your long-term impact on the organization and its people, providing a profound sense of personal fulfillment. Last but not least, taking the time to craft your meaningful legacy not only enhances your reputation as a visionary leader, but also extends your influence beyond your role. This extension of influence empowers you to continue making impactful contributions and garnering recognition for your work in whatever areas or ways you choose to move forward.

Principles and Strategies for Crafting an Enduring Legacy

Reviewing each of the bullets below will help you consider how to begin crafting an enduring legacy for your company – even if you intend to remain at the helm for many years. Legacies are not built overnight or on a whim: They involve plenty of purposeful planning.

> **Align Your Legacy with Vision and Values: This is where your journey begins. Define your purpose** with clarity and intention. Consider how you want your leadership to be remembered, whether it's through innovation, culture, or social responsibility. This is the foundation of your enduring legacy.
>
> **Embed Your Values**: Institutionalize your values in the organization's mission, policies, and daily practices to ensure they endure.

Empower Future Leaders: Your team is your greatest asset. Find them, nurture them, and watch them grow. Resist the urge to micro-manage. Instead, trust in the independence you grant, and encourage them to test it. This is how you empower future leaders, showing them that you believe in their potential.

Plan Succession Thoughtfully: Identify those leaders within your organization who align with your vision and uphold your values.

Mentor Potential Leaders: Dedicate time to mentoring individuals who can carry forward your leadership philosophy.

Cultivate Shared Leadership: This concept promotes a collaborative environment and encourages contributions from all levels. Build an environment where leadership is distributed, enabling contributions from all levels.

Think Long-Term: Prioritize initiatives that secure the organization's future rather than focusing solely on immediate outcomes.

Foster Innovation: Innovation is the lifeblood of any enduring legacy. Establish systems that encourage experimentation, creativity, and continuous improvement. This is where the excitement lies, in the potential for new ideas and the motivation to constantly improve.

Promote Diversity: Build an inclusive culture that values diverse perspectives to ensure adaptability and relevance.

Institutionalize Your Impact: This ensures the sustainability of your legacy. Build scalable systems. Design processes that deliver consistent and sustainable results.

Measure Impact: Define metrics to evaluate the effectiveness of legacy-focused initiatives.

Engage the Broader Community: Strengthen your organization's societal and industry influence through partnerships and outreach.

Envision the Future: Articulate a clear and inspiring vision for the organization's next 20, or 50 years.

Collaborate with Stakeholders: Co-create this vision with employees, board members, and external partners.

Strengthen Stakeholder Ecosystems: Foster strong relationships with customers, investors, and partners.

Leave a Cultural Legacy: Ensure your leadership philosophy becomes part of the organization's DNA.

Document Proven Practices: Share insights and strategies contributing to your leadership impact.

Establish Traditions: Create rituals or events that reflect the organization's values and celebrate its achievements.

Recognize Contributions: Publicly acknowledge the efforts of teams and individuals who embody your legacy.

Key Takeaways for CEOs

Legacy Requires Intentionality: Building a meaningful legacy demands focus, reflection, and action.

Empower Future Leaders: Grooming the next generation is not just a task, it's a responsibility that ensures your vision continues to thrive.

Sustainability is Essential: It's not just about creating systems and cultures, it's about creating ones that are designed for longevity and continuity.

Balance Vision with Execution: Ground your aspirations in tangible results.

> **Define Your Impact**: Your legacy is the lasting mark of your leadership on the organization, its people, and the world. It's a source of pride and satisfaction, a testament to your hard work and dedication.

By embracing these principles, CEOs can ensure that their impact not only endures but continues to inspire and influence future generations. Your legacy will be the ultimate reflection of your leadership philosophy and purpose -- make it one that stands the test of time.

Epilogue

The CEO's Playbook for the Future:

Honing Perceptive Talents and Trusting Them

As you turn the final pages of this guide, know that you are better equipped with strategies, insights, and tools to excel in a business world that demands resilience and innovation.

Leadership today transcends the pursuit of profits; it is about creating meaningful impact, inspiring those around you, and building organizations that thrive in uncertainty while staying anchored in purpose.

Authentic leadership requires a heightened sense of perception -- an ability to deeply understand people, anticipate trends, and make sound decisions rooted in integrity. It's a journey of continuous refinement, where trusting your instincts and honing your perceptive talents are vital for creating lasting value.

The most impactful leaders embrace lifelong learning, foster ethical leadership, empower the next generation, and lead with empathy and vision.

Critical Takeaways for Perceptive Leadership

Stay Curious: The future belongs to leaders who continuously question, explore and adapt. For instance, you can set aside time each week to read about emerging trends in your industry, attend industry conferences, network with other leaders and engage in discussions with your team about potential areas for innovation. Make it a priority to stay informed, sharpen your skills, and seek fresh perspectives.

Model a Learning Culture: Inspire your organization to prioritize curiosity, innovation, and adaptability. When learning is valued at every level, it becomes the engine of transformation.

Refine Perceptive Talents: Hone your ability to sense emerging opportunities, identify challenges, and interpret subtle shifts in the business landscape. Do this by bringing all your senses into the equation: What are you seeing? Hearing? Smelling and tasting? (Yes! Smelling & tasting depending on your business!) Touching? Bring all this sensory subjective knowledge to the mix with objective thinking to find new ideas and pathways forward.

Add the Data: There's so much information for you to consider and artificial intelligence (AI) is making it easier than ever to gather everything from quick insight to complex research. Use the technological tools available and keep humanity in the mix.

Anchor in Values: Let your principles guide your actions, particularly during times of uncertainty. Decisions rooted in ethics build trust and credibility and ensure a sense of security and respect among your team and stakeholders. Ask yourself: How will I feel about these decisions a year from now? Or even 20 years from now?

Foster Transparency: Open communication and accountability create strong connections with employees, customers, and stakeholders. Trust your perceptive instincts to know when deeper dialogue is needed. Then, open the conversations with a sincere objective of learning and growing forward.

Lead with Integrity: The strength of your leadership lies in making choices that align with your moral compass and long-term vision. Leading with integrity should give you a sense of confidence and security in your decision-making process.

Empower the Next Generation: Your legacy is not just about your achievements, but also about the leaders you inspire. By dedicating time to mentoring future leaders who will continue your mission, you empower them and instill a sense of hope and optimism for the future of your organization.

Create Development Pathways: Offer growth opportunities, encouraging your team to take initiative and innovate. By investing in their growth and success, you can trust their abilities while guiding their development, fostering a sense of mutual investment and growth.

Cultivate Trust: Perceptive CEOs understand their people's potential and create an environment where talent can flourish.

Lead by Listening: Prioritize your team's needs and well-being. Empathy and humility are the characteristics of the best leaders. You're still the boss. You will make the decisions. But listening first can prevent lots of headaches, issues and problems.

Serve Before You Lead: Focus on empowering others and creating conditions for their success rather than seeking personal accolades.

Build Relationships: Deepen your perceptive abilities by understanding your team's motivations, fears, and aspirations. Likewise, do this for yourself by aligning with mentors who can support and encourage your personal growth.

Prepare for Change: Resilience comes from anticipating disruptions and embedding adaptability into your organization's culture.

Align with Purpose: Lead with a vision that balances your business goals with social and environmental impact. Purpose-driven organizations stand the test of time.

Trust Perceptive Insights: Use your ability to sense shifts and trends to stay ahead of the curve and align your strategy with future needs.

A Call to Action: Lead into the Future with Vision and Trust

The future needs perceptive leaders who adapt with agility, inspire authentically, and confidently lead. As a CEO, your unique position allows you to shape your organization and the industries, communities, and societies you influence.

To do this today and all your days at the helm of whatever company you lead…remember these final points.

- **Hone Your Perceptive Talents**: Develop the ability to read between the lines, anticipate challenges, and see opportunities others overlook.
- **Trust Your Instincts**: Cultivate confidence in your decision-making by combining deep knowledge with intuitive insights.
- **Inspire Change**: Use your leadership to foster equity, sustainability, and innovation in the world around you.
- **Empower Others**: Share your vision, trust your team, and guide them in ways that unlock their potential.

Your journey as a CEO is a privilege and a responsibility. It is not defined solely by the profits you generate but by the lives you touch, the values you uphold, and the legacy you create.

Leadership is a constant evolution of your perceptive abilities and your ability to trust them to guide you in times of complexity.

The playbook is now in your hands. Lead boldly, trust deeply, and shape a future filled with purpose and impact. The future awaits -- and you are ready to lead it.

Lastly, along the way, if you want a thought partner and sounding board you can confide in to gain perspective, enhance decision-making, and develop additional leadership strategies, let's talk. You already have many of the answers. I bring the questions to help you find those answers so you can make decisions more confidently, move forward boldly, and become the ultimate leader and peak performer you were born to be.

About the Author

For over 30 years, Dian Griesel has served as a confidential advisor and strategist to C-suite leaders of private and publicly traded companies as well as venture capital funds, specializing in shareholder, stakeholder and media dynamics. With a keen ability to read between the lines, she provides invaluable insights into the unseen and unsaid aspects of complex conversations and events — internal and external — that influence negotiations and the reception of critical announcements.

From navigating crises and funding transactions to managing leadership changes and stakeholder disclosures, Dian is known for developing and delivering actionable strategies to ensure clarity, compliance, and strategic alignment. With a deep understanding of FDA, FTC, SEC, and DOD regulations, she has helped clients avoid costly missteps while maintaining trust during pivotal moments.

In addition to private consulting, Dian leads onsite lectures and workshops that explore how beliefs and perceptions shape relationships, interactions, and decision-making. She also collaborates with a team of seasoned public relations executives to craft thought leadership opportunities and manage high-stakes communications.

Dian's credentials include a Ph.D. in Health Sciences, Corporate Governance Certification from The Wharton School, and certification as a consulting hypnotherapist (Union 472; NFH 104). As a member of the American Counseling Association and a lifetime member of the International Association of Counselors & Therapists, she brings a unique perspective to her corporate and private client work. Dian is also the author of 15 books on topics ranging from investor relations and public relations to self-awareness and health. Additionally, she hosts the top-ranking *Perception Dynamics Silver Disobedience* podcast and has built a blog readership of nearly 1 million monthly readers (Google/Meta stats).

From 2012 to mid-2024, she led DGI, a PR firm specializing in thought leadership and premium content production. Before that, Dian founded The Investor Relations Group, an IR and PR firm, which she sold to an investment bank in 2012. Dian's career began in talent management, representing iconic comedians like Jay Leno, Bill Maher, and Jerry Seinfeld—a testament to her lifelong appreciation for the power of connection and humor.

If you're curious to learn more, you can learn more in the links below.

Lots more info here: https://diangriesel.com
or here: https://www.linkedin.com/in/diangriesel/
or here: https://www.psychologytoday.com/profile/450545

Made in the USA
Las Vegas, NV
28 February 2025

18860758R00155